Teaching Kids to Care & Cooperate

50 Easy Writing, Discussion & Art Activities That Help Develop Self-Esteem, Responsibility, & Respect for Others

Kathy Pike

Jean Mumper

Alice Fiske

We're a Great Bunch

SCHOLASTIC
PROFESSIONAL BOOKS

NEW YORK • TORONTO • LONDON • AUCKLAND • SYDNEY
MEXICO CITY • NEW DELHI • HONG KONG

DEDICATION

To all the children, their families, and our colleagues who have enriched our lives.

Kathy, Jean, and Alice

ACKNOWLEDGMENTS

Our deepest appreciation to all the "community" members who made this book possible—our families, our students, the editors at Scholastic, and the teachers whose classrooms are represented in this book. Writing a book about creating caring classrooms proved to us that we are all connected and that everyone plays an important part when designing effective educational experiences and establishing a supportive atmosphere for learning.

Dear Children of the Earth: A Letter from Home by Schim Schimmel.
Published by Shogakukan Inc. Used by permission of the publisher and the author.

Cover design by Norma Ortiz and Kelli Thompson
Cover artwork by Danielle Blood and Rebecca Callan
Interior design by Solutions by Design, Inc.
Interior illustrations by the authors, with additional artwork by the
students and teachers of their respective school communities.
Edited by Elaine Israel

ISBN: 0-439-09849-1

Table of Contents

Introduction 6

CHAPTER ONE
To Build a Community 7
    Send a Letter 8
    From Student to Student 8
    Whose Favorite Books Are These? 8
    Find Someone Who… 9
    Student Résumés 10
    Quilts for the Year 11
    The Meaning of Community 12

CHAPTER TWO
A Class Democracy 13
    Class Meetings 13
    Sharing Responsibilities 15
    Activities for Each Month 17
    Bring on Literature 21
    A Room of Their Own 21
    Biographical Posters 21
    Brown Bag It! 22
    Bulletin Board Bunch 22
    I Messages 22
    Body Maps and Silhouettes 23
    Name Mural 24
    Time Lines Tell Tales 24
    Pages in Our Lives 27
    All About Me From A to Z 28
    Student of the Week 28
    We All Measure Up 28
    Me Books 29
    Getting to Know You Quilt 30

CHAPTER THREE
The Community Rules 31
    Rules for Living and Learning 31
    Now That You Have Them, What Do You Do With Class Rules? 33

Class Bill of Rights 33
T and Y Charts 35
Solving Problems 36
Words of Conflict 37
Chat to Mr. Tuttle 38
All the Room's a Stage 38
Student-Designed Handbooks 39
Student Court 40
Think Positively 41
Pillowcase Quilt 42

CHAPTER FOUR
Accentuate the Positive

Accentuate the Positive 43
Good News Notes 43
Happy Thoughts 44
Send Home Newsletters 44
A Marble for Your Thoughts 45
Showcase Accomplishments 46
Set Goals 46
Budding Journalists 47
Book It 47
Throw Bouquets 47
Good-Deed Book 48
Thank-You Quilt 48

CHAPTER FIVE
Ripples of Kindness

Ripples of Kindness 49
Kindness Matters 49
Kindness Journals 50
The Thoughtful Box 50
Kindness Learning Center 50
Using Technology 52
Countdown to RAK Week 52
Winding Down on a High Note 52
Kindness Activities 53
You Can Make a Difference 54
Lend a Hand 54
Friends Always 54
Accentuate the Negative? 55
Six Friendly Things to Do 55
Kind Deeds Quilt 56

CHAPTER SIX
Beyond the Classroom 59
Bulletin Board 60
What Would Our World Be Like? 60
The Earth at Our Fingertips: Pollution 61
Looking Out 62
Environmental Education 63
Packaging for Eternity? 64
Environmental Word Walls 65
12 Ways to Extend Your Study 65
Earth Day Journals 66

CHAPTER SEVEN
Caring for Other People 67
Peaceful Moments 67
Community of Peacemakers 68
Classmates Near and Far 69

CHAPTER EIGHT
Time to Celebrate 71
Units and Celebrations 71
Dr. Seuss's Birthday 76
The 100th Day 76
Math Month/Family Math Night 77
Poetry Month 77
Celebrate Book-Award Winners 78
The Great Nutrition Adventure 78
The Olympics 79
Celebrate Children 79
Year-End Performance 79
Growing Together 80
Corkstrip Quilt 81

REPRODUCIBLES 82

Bibliography 89

Introduction

This book is about creating a classroom in which every child is celebrated not only as an individual but also as part of the whole classroom community. We intend our suggestions to be guides that will help you create a caring, responsive classroom. Our theme is that we are all connected.

We want this book to help you with classroom management and discipline as part of an ongoing class program in both the affective and cognitive domains. Many of the activities build or sustain class community as well as support learning in a variety of curriculums. Because we believe so strongly in the power of literature, we have also included an extensive bibliography after the last chapter.

You do not need a special occasion to celebrate harmony, caring, and concern for others and the environment. But some special occasions, such as Martin Luther King Jr. Day, Make a Difference Day, Random Acts of Kindness Week, and Earth Day, lend themselves to events that show how we are connected; we have included many activities for them.

We hope you will find this resource invaluable throughout this school year and for many school years to come.

Kathy Pike, Jean Mumper, and Alice Fiske

CHAPTER ONE

To Build a Community

COMMUNITY a group of people living together or sharing common interests and pursuits; a small supportive group that symbolizes belonging.

Children learn best in a classroom and school that are safe and caring places, places where a premium is set on academic achievement. Their foundation is a community that extends beyond classroom walls and beyond school grounds. Building such a community is an ongoing process.

A class community is a lot like an orchestra. Its members produce harmonious music together because each makes an individual contribution. Just as the conductor of an orchestra is responsible for the final quality of its performance, so is the teacher responsible for the quality of his or her classroom. You, the teacher, are the catalyst who structures the daily routines and develops the expectations for both learning and behavior. As you establish the groundwork, students assume more responsibility, and participate in designing what they learn and how they learn it.

In the ideal classroom community, students consider, care for, encourage, and academically support one another. In the ideal school community, teachers, students, parents, and other members enjoy mutual respect. In a school that has a culture of caring, you will find trust, openness, acceptance, responsibility, self-evaluation, and self-discipline on the part of the students and the teachers. Here, teachers listen to their students, value what they say, and show their appreciation. Teachers also provide opportunities for children to learn responsibility and to practice self-discipline.

Send a Letter

Begin building your classroom community even before the school year starts. Children love to receive mail, so what better way to welcome them and to introduce yourself than with a letter or postcard you've mailed over the summer. Include greetings, a list of needed supplies, a short description of your expectations, highlights of the coming year, and some information about yourself.

From Student to Student

On the first day of school, greet students with notes from, and perhaps photographs of, former students. (If you can possibly do it, match current students with those who had the same desks the year before.) The new arrivals will love the notes, which ease first-day jitters and give insights into the upcoming year.

At the end of one school year, Diane Zeiset asked her fourth graders to write notes to the next year's class, telling them what to expect. Some students advised the incoming class to be prepared with extra pencils, stressed the importance of writing down assignments, and noted that the teacher particularly likes coated chocolate candies!

Whose Favorite Books Are These?

Your school librarian can help to introduce the faculty to new students. Each teacher in the school should choose the jacket of a favorite book and, on medium-sized index cards, explain why he or she chose that particular book—without revealing any identities.

The librarian can display the jackets and the cards, with a master list of the participating teachers nearby. Challenge students to match each teacher with the right book. Reward books to students who correctly make all the matches or get a high percentage correct.

Find Someone Who...

Did you ever notice how quiet the first day of school is, when everyone is still a little shy and not quite sure what to expect? Well, Find Someone Who... allows classmates to get to know one another. Just provide each student with a sheet of paper on which are listed a myriad of activities and interests.

Find Someone Who...

vacationed outside the state this summer.   _____

has a pet.   _____

read a science fiction book this summer.   _____

had a birthday over the summer.   _____

likes to in-line skate.   _____

loves pizza.   _____

took lessons this summer.   _____

has a birthday in the same month as you.   _____

The children go around the room asking classmates if they have a pet, love pizza, and so on. The questioners write their classmates' names or initials in the correct spot. To make sure the entire class is involved, each student can be listed only once.

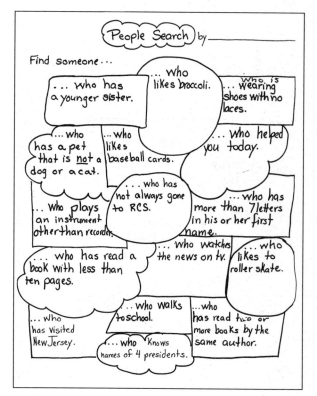

Variations

This activity is also handy for PTSA or parent meetings. It can be used with any subject area as a way to tap into prior knowledge or to help students review and study for a test collaboratively. You just have to write questions that deal with a topic (rain forests, the American Revolution, math facts, for example). Students go around the classroom, asking questions of their classmates. For example, if the topic is U.S. Presidents, ask students to **Find a President Who...**

freed the slaves.   _____
served in the Armed Forces.   _____
was impeached.   _____
never lived in the White House.   _____

Invite students to create their own versions for the class to use as a review for a subject they are studying.

Student Résumés

Ask your students to fill out résumés that provide information on interests, hobbies, travels, goals, likes, and dislikes. Instead of a résumé format, provide a personal profile template on which children can tell about their favorites (foods, television shows, movies, sports), likes and dislikes about school, goals, items they would place in a time capsule, and leisure activities. Place the profiles in a class book or directory for posterity.

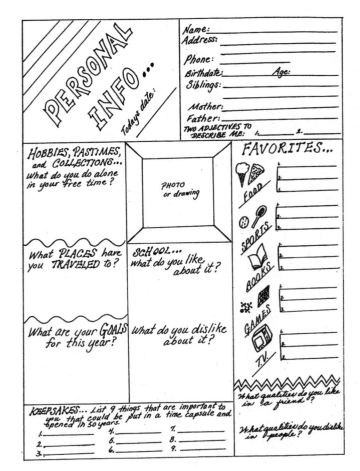

Quilts for the Year

We've threaded quilt-making activities throughout the book to encourage kids to join together and celebrate their commonalities—to connect.

We'll Piece Together a Wonderful Year

Alice Fiske likes to use the message We'll Piece Together a Wonderful Year to greet her children on the first day of school. This has become her theme and the center message of a quilt for her third graders. She surrounds the words with a border of different quilt squares—one for each child in the class—to show that each child is both unique and part of the class community. Alice's children talk about how it takes many small patches and pieces to create a whole quilt. Their year together becomes like a patchwork quilt as they add many pieces to form a whole.

Alice's Special Quilt

Alice has a tradition. Every year, she shares her personal first-day-of-school quilt with her new class. The quilt is made of patches from each first-day-of-school outfit Alice wore during her own school years. The clothes were lovingly made by her grandmother. As her class sits on the floor around the quilt, Alice tells stories of her first days and how quilts can be windows into the past.

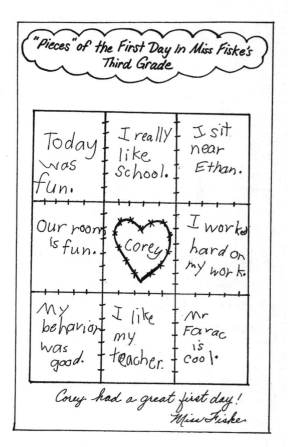

"Pieces" of the First Day in Miss Fiske's Third Grade

Today was fun.

I really like school.

I sit near Ethan.

Our room is fun.

Corey

I worked hard on my work.

My behavior was good.

I like my teacher.

Mr Farac is cool.

Corey had a great first day!
Miss Fiske

   After learning about Alice's quilt, her class uses a simple patch pattern, like the ones used by pioneer children, to create a quilt like the one at right. Alice gives each student a sheet of paper on which to draw a quiltlike square. In the square, each child describes his or her thoughts and feelings about the first day of the new school year. If you do this activity, you may want to add your comments along the bottom of the sheet or on the square itself. This is an excellent way to inform parents about what was important to their children on the first day. Add the completed quilt squares to the students' portfolios.

Community Quilt

The fifth-grade students in Therese Gilbert's class constructed a community quilt that reflected their harmonious classroom. The children chose a topic to represent caring, respect, and responsibility and used a variety of materials, such as fabric paint, felt, and scraps of fabric, to design their squares. A parent assisted in the assembly of the quilt, which the class proudly hung in their room.

Ms. Gilbert's Class Community Quilt xxx

The Meaning of COMMUNITY

Here's how some of our fifth graders define it.

In the past semester, I've learned a lot about community. Community means people working together as a team and caring for each other. It also means friends and family having fun. It means getting together and getting things done. Community is people sharing and caring and forgiving everyone.
    Lucas

Community mostly means caring for each other. That means helping, sharing, and having fun with each other.
    Jill

I think community is a great thing. Community is all about caring, loving, helping, and friendship. I learned good things about communities. Community is a great way of getting friends and working together. I love being in my classroom community and my home community.
    Ludovica

A community could be anywhere—in your house, school, and many more places.
    Jennifer

CHAPTER TWO

A Class Democracy

Draw parallels between the rules, responsibilities, and privileges that children might have at home with those they have in school. In a sense, the home is a community and a class is like a family. In their journals, students could describe what they think it takes to be a member of a class community. With students' permission, share these entries at a class meeting and develop them as a rights and responsibilities chart. (More on this later in this chapter.)

Routines, procedures, attitudes, and activities evolve over time as teachers and their students learn to trust one another. Children learn democracy by living it, and classrooms should provide opportunities for them to grow into responsible citizens. They need to be given ownership for managing many of the classroom routines and must be involved in the class's daily decision making. Some ways of doing this, which are detailed in this chapter:

- Hold regular class meetings.

- Assign responsibilities.

- Plan whole class activities.

- Collaborate on a room design.

Class Meetings

Class meetings go beyond the typical circle time, during which academic subjects are the prime focus. Class meetings can take place every day or once a week, and at any time.

Sitting in a circle works best because everyone can be seen and heard. Use chairs rather than floor seating to help the meeting seem more official and keep the kids focused. But if you prefer the informality of sitting on the floor, do it!

You can't just start class meetings and expect them to be effective and productive right off the bat. You need time to set the tone for the year and to establish relationships among the people taking part. At the start of the school year, class meetings serve mainly as a way for students to become better acquainted. As the year progresses, the meetings will serve as a forum for addressing problems.

Topics for Class Meetings

GENERAL BEHAVIOR

- in the halls
- in line
- in the cafeteria

TEAM PLAY

- following rules at recess
- including classmates in activities
- choosing teams for recess games

CLASSROOM PROTOCOL

- teasing
- sharing computer time
- caring for the classroom

Alice sets aside three days a week for her third-grade class to hold meetings. If there's a situation that needs to be dealt with immediately, she makes time for a discussion even if it's not a regular day.

Several students are assigned to be discussion leaders, and it is their responsibility to plan the agenda and raise issues. Alice sets aside time on the discussion day (or the day before) for students to plan together. Until they are ready to assume total responsibility, she meets with them to review their plan and to discuss effective presentation and discussion techniques. Alice has found that classroom concerns receive prime billing at the beginning of the school year, but as the year progresses and the students become more confident in their skills, the topics become more complex, often dealing with the school community and global issues, such as ecology, the environment, and politics.

On the two days that have no planned discussions, the children focus on current events gleaned from newspapers or publications like *Scholastic News*. There's always time for student sharing and a read-aloud.

In Jean's fifth-grade classroom, students are encouraged to jot on self-sticking notes their problems or their concerns about the class community. The notes are folded for privacy and firmly stuck on Jean's plan book. That way they will not be lost or overlooked. Jean's students sign their names, which may or may not come up during the discussions. As teachers know, what may seem insignificant may be quite important to a child. If you feel greater care about privacy is needed, you may want to place a secure suggestion box on your desk.

Sharing Responsibilities

As educators, we want to help and encourage students to be independent. One way to foster independence is to have them share in the caretaking and management of the classroom. As with adults, sharing responsibilities is important for children. The more responsibilities they assume, the greater their sense of ownership of their space and the deeper their feelings of community. During the school year, you can watch and listen for ideas about what types of jobs or responsibilities will help make your classroom more communal. All the children in Alice Fiske's class have jobs. Here are some of them.

Title: Shelves and Centers Organizer
Description: organizes supplies and keeps shelves orderly

Title: Librarian
Description: After the first child to have this job is trained by the teacher, the children train one another to maintain the library and reference books in the classroom media center.

Title: Lunch-Count Helper
Description: keeps track of lunch orders and records them on a slip to send to the cafeteria

Title: Line Leader and Line Ender
Description: Work together to keep the class lines in order in the halls. They assign points to the class for hall behavior, which are later traded in for rewards.

Title: Errand Person
Description: runs errands for the teacher

Title: Supplies Helper
Description: distributes supplies for project, passes out books or folders

Title: Mail Person
Description: distributes mail to student mailboxes in the classroom, passes out corrected papers, notes to go home, and notes to students; and is responsible for making sure that all material is distributed by the end of the day

Title: Chair Monitor
Description: clears away all empty chairs in the morning and returns them to their places at the end of the day

Alice's classroom management scheme is called Each Person's Piece Is Important. She uses the community quilt, described at the end of chapter one as a job chart. Around the edge of the quilt pieces, Alice places magnetic cards on which are written the classroom job titles. Every week, Alice moves the cards one space. That takes care of remembering who has done what! The students can easily see what their next jobs will be and when favorite jobs will again come their way.

Variation

To help her second graders assume some responsibility for the cleanliness and appearance of their classroom, Barbara Johnson gives a child the job of cubby master for the week. Because the cubbies are in a hallway outside the room, they are visible to anyone who passes. At the end of the day, the cubby master inspects the cubbies and informs students if they have to straighten them before going home. The result is that the children develop a sense of pride in keeping their school neat.

In lower grades, the word *job* is commonly used. In upper grades, *responsibilities* may be more appropriate because the word seems to emphasize the importance of each task.

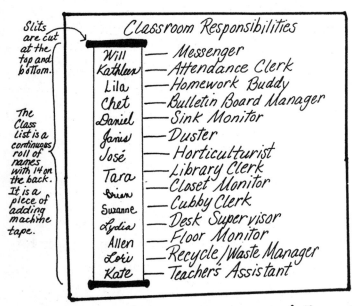

Slits are cut at the top and bottom.

The Class List is a continuous roll of names with 14 on the back. It is a piece of adding machine tape.

Classroom Responsibilities

Will — Messenger
Kathleen — Attendance Clerk
Lila — Homework Buddy
Chet — Bulletin Board Manager
Daniel — Sink Monitor
Janis — Duster
José — Horticulturist
Tara — Library Clerk
Brian — Closet Monitor
Suzanne — Cubby Clerk
Lydia — Desk Supervisor
Allen — Floor Monitor
Lori — Recycle/Waste Manager
Kate — Teacher's Assistant

Classroom Task Management Board

Who Does What?

MATERIALS

- ☆ a large piece of cardboard or poster board
- ☆ roll of adding-machine tape
- ☆ permanent marker
- ☆ cellophane tape or glue

STEPS

1. On the cardboard, leave enough room at the left margin to accommodate the width of adding machine tape.

2. At the left margin, make two slits, each wide enough for the adding machine tape. One slit is about two inches from the top of the cardboard. The other is about two inches up from the bottom.

3. Cut the tape to twice the length of the cardboard, so that it can be connected to make a continuous loop.

4. Place students' names spaced about two inches apart on the tape.

5. Laminate the list once you've placed all the names. Add new students' names with permanent marker. If students leave, cut the paper, remove the name, and retape.

6. Thread the list into the two slits and use cellophane tape or glue to attach the two ends.

7. Roll the listing so that each student has a chance to assume each responsibility on a weekly basis.

Activities for Each Month

As we dash from one part of our lives to another, we need gentle reminders that we are part of a community. This is especially true for a class whose spirit of community is fragmented by pullouts, special lessons, and other activities. Yet it is possible to build a connected community in nontraditional ways throughout the year.

For example, Alice's third-grade class does monthly projects. Like any activity, not all the ideas here will work with all groups at all times. But even doing a few will reinforce the theme of being connected.

In **September**, the students make paper images of themselves in their first-day-of-school clothes. Everyone begins with a sheet of paper that is the same size. But the results prove that the class is made up of many individuals. When the figures are displayed hand to hand, they remind us of how different, yet connected, we all are.

In **October**, the students draw pumpkins. Again the children each start with a

sheet of paper the same size. Soon this lesson on symmetry has each child cutting a pumpkin, each with a different size and shape. When the shapes are placed side by side and are joined by a vine, the class can see that "in our patch, we are all connected."

November is the time to share feelings of thankfulness. Students cut feather shapes out of colored paper. Again, the exercise starts with the same size and shape and ends with a variety. This time, though, the children write a few words or sentences telling what they are particularly thankful for. The feathers are joined together on a simple turkey body to form a hall display, Our Class Is Joined in Thankfulness.

By **December**, the children are catching on to Alice's plan and wonder how they'll be connected this time. Out come the scissors and the brown paper. Again, the class begins with the same size paper. This time, the instruction is to fold it and cut a triangle. The results are, as with the other projects, varied. The triangles are turned into reindeer; the scraps become ears and horns. Then a bright red piece of yarn is used to join together the reindeer team.

Hopes and Dreams

As part of a **January** unit on Martin Luther King Jr., children draw self-portraits using a generic body shape. It is the students' job to make their portraits unique. Once the portraits are complete, they are joined together, hand in hand with speech bubbles stating their hopes and dreams for a better world.

February is a great time to celebrate Random Acts of Kindness Week. This time, children trace their hands, writing a positive word about themselves on each finger. Join the hands to form a peace sign. Place it on a magnetic white board or shape it into a wreath to be placed on the door of your room. Add hearts with the children's names.

March is the time for a national initiative, Read Across America, which encourages parents and their children to read together. Because the focus of this activity is reading, the finished product is a bookmark.

Bookmarks

MATERIALS

☆ a piece of rectangular shaped piece of paper for each child

☆ scissors

☆ two feet of yarn or ribbon for each child

STEPS (for children)

1. Cut off the top two corners so it has a roof-like appearance.

2. Punch a hole in the center of the top of the paper so yarn or ribbon can be pulled through to create a tassel.

3. To make the tassel, fold the yarn in half and pull it through the hole to create a loop about one inch long.

4. Draw the two ends over the top and through the loop.

5. Pull the ends to tighten the tassel.

6. Decorate the bookmarks with reading slogans, drawings, pictures from magazines, stickers, or rubber stamps.

7. Connect each end of one tassel to another to create a bookmark chain. The bookmarks could surround or be curved above a large book shape bearing such titles as Reading Joins Us Together and Marking Our Way Through Reading.

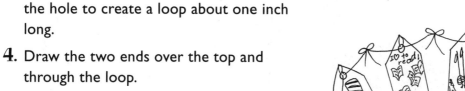

Directions for bookmark tassel

To make bookmark tassel, feed yarn or ribbon loop through hole and pass loose ends through loop. Pull to tighten.

Earth Day is in **April**. Use the concept of Heart and Hand as you encourage the class to think about caring for Earth. The children begin with pieces of red paper (all the same size) folded in half, from which they can cut out symmetrical hearts. So many different hearts result from these simple directions! On the hearts, ask students to write one thing that they will put their hearts into doing for Earth (don't pollute, pick up litter, recycle, for example). Use the hands you made in February to help form the display for Join Our Hearts and Hands Around Our Earth.

What does **May** bring? Spring flowers that bloom in your room!

May Flowers

MATERIALS

☆ a long, thin piece of 3"x12" white paper for each child

☆ a black crayon for each child

☆ green, yellow, red, and orange watercolor paints

☆ a square piece of 4"x4" white paper for each child

STEPS (for the children)

1. Draw a long, thin stem on the paper.

2. Draw five to seven leaves attached to the stem.

3. Trace around the stem and leaves with black crayon.

4. Use a wash of green and yellow watercolor paints to fill in the stem and leaves.

5. Draw a circle in the center of the square paper. Add petals around the circle.

6. Trace the circle and the petals with black crayon.

7. Use a wash of yellow, red, and orange watercolors to fill in the flowers.

8. Once the paint is dry, cut out and assemble the parts.

Same size papers…same directions…same colors…but what a difference in the flowers! Create a lovely unique garden under the heading We're All Growing in This Class or This Class Gives Us Roots. To make the title more personal, use your name or the class name in place of the generic word *class*.

All good things must come to an end, which is why **June** is such a bittersweet month. Still, saying so long for now to friends is tempered by the thought of summer vacation. The connection this month will be lighthearted. The headings could be: Sailing Into Summer or Sailing on to 4th Grade.

A fleet of sailboats joined by ocean waves will give everyone a sense of sailing into the sunset after a wonderful year. Start with the same size paper (of course!), this time a rectangle of 4" x 8" white paper, which students turn into a boat shape by cutting a triangle off two sides—two diagonal cuts from the top corners to the bottom edges (no scraps!). The two triangular pieces, glued to

Caring
responsible
athletic
intelligent
giving

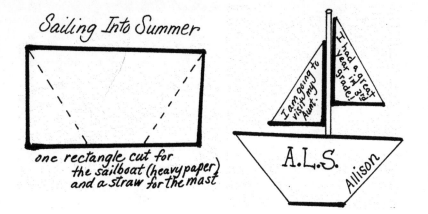

Sailing Into Summer

one rectangle cut for the sailboat (heavy paper) and a straw for the mast

A.L.S.

Allison

I am going to visit my Aunt.

I had a great year in 3rd grade!

either side of a mast (an ice cream stick or a straw), become the sails. Students can write good-bye messages or summer plans on the sails.

When they are completed, everyone can note the diversity of the boats. No doubt about it! The class is indeed connected.

Bring on Literature

Once children realize how connected they are, it's so much easier to discuss a shared story or to accept other points of view. Literature can, of course, be a powerful way to reinforce the concept of connection. Choose an appropriate novel from the extensive bibliography at the end of this book.

A Room of Their Own

Encourage your students to decorate their classroom. This doesn't mean that a completely empty room should greet them when they start classes for the year. You need to do some decorating to make the room welcoming. But as the year goes on, the children should have a role in deciding how their surroundings look.

Here are some art ideas to get you started.

Biographical Posters

They say "Here's who I am and where I'm from." Some items that can be artfully arranged on a large piece of poster board include:

- photographs of family, pets, and trips
- magazine pictures depicting interests and hobbies
- a photocopy of birth certificate
- a family tree
- awards
- footprints and handprints
- pressed flowers or leaves from the student's backyard or neighborhood
- a map showing where family members were born

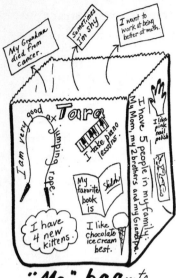

"Me" bag...to reflect inside and outside feelings and interests

Brown Bag It!

Using an ordinary lunch or grocery bag, students may give you and their classmates insights into what makes them tick. Students decorate the outside of their bags with pictures, drawings, and photographs that have some meaning to them. Inside, students can place slightly more personal items, such as a list of goals for the year, and even more personal thoughts— wishes, fears, favorite things to do—written on small cards.

Bulletin Board Bunch

To emphasize the positive aspects of each class member, Judy Russert's fourth graders created a bulletin board for the school showcase. The students constructed a large flower with their names at the center. On the stem and leaves were comments from Judy and her students, with each child describing positive things about a classmate. Here are a few of them.

Nicole shares well. (from Katherine)
Nicole is good at leading the group. (Lenny)
Kaylah is good at writing. (Lawrence)
Kaylah is a good listener. (Buddy)
I like the way you give people pencils. (Tim)
Delaney is willing to help others. (Tiffany)
She gets all her work done. (Josh)
Lawrence is a good problem solver. (Mrs. Russert)

Once your class starts to evolve into a community, its members might want to get to know more about one another. The following projects, which can be done at school or at home, reveal students' interests, hopes, fears, and dreams (if the students wish them to be revealed).

We're a Great Bunch

I Messages

Knowing how to express feelings in a way that neither antagonizes nor threatens is an invaluable skill. I Messages are perfect for this purpose. An I Message is a way a student can respond to a situation or to others' behavior. It communicates feelings in a way that allows the other person to avoid becoming defensive or evasive.

To make the concept of I Messages clear, it helps to practice using them.

Provide verbal (or written) prompts or formats so that students can phrase their concerns. For example:

I feel upset (frustrated, sad) when _____.
I don't like it (get frustrated) when you _____ because _____.
I feel _____ when _____.

I Messages can express positive feelings as well. For example:
I feel great because you _____.
I appreciate _____ because _____.
I feel happy when _____.

Body Maps and Silhouettes

Body maps and silhouettes are outlines of a child's body shape on which you can record information about that child. Body maps can be life-size, with an actual tracing of the child's body, or they can be a generic body shape (about two to three feet tall works well). Younger children may be more comfortable with body tracing than older, self-conscious students. Once the children are given their body maps, they fill in the shapes with pictures (original or from magazines), words, quotes—anything that tells about them.

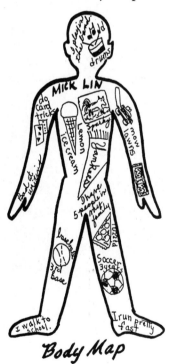

Body Map

During class meetings, discuss the significance of the objects they placed on their body maps, providing yet another way for the students to get to know one another. If you like, place the finished artwork around the room or drape them onto chairs to greet visitors at open houses.

You could also trace the students' silhouettes or use a generic silhouette. Students can fill in their silhouettes with similar information. The silhouette can become the cover for an autobiography or an All About Me book, with individually shaped silhouette pages used for the data and pictures that the children provide. Place these books in the class library for all to enjoy, or give to parents as gifts for holidays or special occasions. The books make excellent pieces to display at parent conferences or at open houses.

Instead of using actual body shapes, you could also use stick figures, with different parts of the figure describing personality traits, feelings, likes, and dislikes. For example:

The head represents a favorite book.
The heart represents feelings about school or an issue.
The hands represent things a student is good at and things the student likes.
The feet stand for dislikes and for areas that need improvement.
The mouth spouts advice to a classmate or to others.

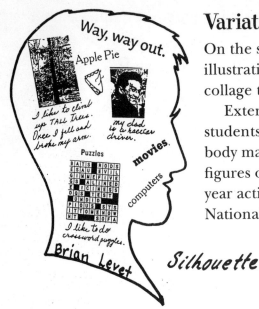

Way, way out.

Apple Pie

I like to climb up TALL Trees. Once I fell and broke my arm.

my dad is a soccer driver.

movies.

Puzzles

computers

I like to do crossword puzzles.

Brian Levet

Silhouette

Variation

On the silhouettes, place words, symbols, pictures, and illustrations that represent students' thoughts. The result is a collage that focuses on their interests.

Extend the silhouettes across the curriculum. For example, students can choose a favorite book character and create a body map for the character. You could also use historical figures or contemporary newsmakers. This is a great end-of-the-year activity to honor books read during the year or as part of National Education Week or Children's Book Week.

Name Mural

The centerpiece of many classrooms is, of course, the main bulletin board. Create one that features the names of children in your room. You could ask children to do their own names or to choose a classmate's name out of a hat. Imagine how many colorful ways names can be illustrated.

To emphasize the theme We all Fit Together, cut a poster board jigsaw-style, with one piece for each person in the room, including you. Each student writes his or her name on a piece and decorates it. Reassemble and display the poster board.

Time Lines Tell Tales

Time lines could be another bulletin-board theme. Have each student do his or her own, starting at birth and going up to and including his or her year in your classroom. Brainstorm a list of dates to include. For example:

◎ a special trip or event

◎ losing the first tooth

◎ arrival of siblings

24

- arrival of pets
- first day of kindergarten
- meeting a special person

As a companion piece to individual time lines, make a **class time line**, too. Ask one child or a committee to keep it up-to-date. Among the events you could highlight are field trips, visits by guest speakers, assemblies, concerts, and state tests. Enrich the time line with local, state, national, and world events. Illustrate with photos or cut-out magazine illustrations. Time lines will help students see their own lives with a different perspective. Invite your students to take time lines one step further. They may enjoy developing their own Stories in a Can and Stories in Cubes.

Variations

Time lines are integral to several curricular areas—social studies, science, and language arts, for example. They can cover the lives of historical figures, the science of making maple syrup or paper, and the history of your state. If your school, town, or state is having a significant anniversary your students may enjoy doing collaborative research on celebratory time lines.

Stories in a Can

MATERIALS

- ☆ soft-sided containers, such as potato-chip and bread-crumb canisters
- ☆ adhesive shelf paper, felt, wallpaper, gift wrap
- ☆ glue
- ☆ lengths of paper cut from long rolls, or individual sheets of paper that are taped together

STEPS

1. Decorate the containers.

2. Make a slit about one quarter of an inch wide the long way down the side of each container.

3. Ask students to write their life stories and time lines. Laminate the paper to make it easier to handle. After each student writes his or her story, roll it up (beginning with the end of the story) and insert into containers.

4. Place the containers in the class library or in an area of the classroom, such as a Class Museum, where they'll be available for all to enjoy.

Stories in Cubes

MATERIALS

☆ half-gallon juice and milk containers (to make each cube more durable, use two cartons for one cube)

☆ plain paper on which students write their information

☆ Here are some ideas for what can be placed on each cube.

a picture or illustration of the student

the student's name in fancy print

lists of hobbies, favorite foods, goals for the year, memorable events, and accomplishments

advice on how to succeed in your grade

a relevant quote

a review of a favorite book

short descriptions of family members and pets

make-believe postcards of memorable vacations

STEPS

1. Cut the cartons so they are six-inch squares. Insert one carton into the other.

2. Cover with plain paper upon which the students' information has been written.

Variations

These cubes make wonderful, concrete graphing tools. Whenever a class graph is to be constructed, instead of using a traditional paper form the cubes can be used. First, the items being graphed are listed, generally on the white board or chalkboard. The students then put their cubes under the item that reflects their choice. For example, students can list some possible favorite after-school pastimes, such as reading, watching TV, and playing a game. Then they place their cubes under the activity that they enjoy most. If desired, small wooden blocks and class composite school pictures can be used to make the cubes. Just paste the individual student pictures onto the small wooden blocks and voilá—another instant concrete way to graph.

Autobiography on a cube

Bags of Stories

Students can house their autobiographical artifacts in any kind of holder—a briefcase, shoe box, small suitcase, or canvas bag, for example. To give ideas about what kind of artifacts could be included, model your own autobiography in a bag. For example, Kathy uses these eight items to give insights into her life:

1. a figurine of a boy reading (to represent her three sons and her chosen profession in the reading field)

2. a pair of sneakers (representing her love of running)

3. a plastic rooster (as a reminder of a favorite bedtime story her Russian grandmother told her)

4. a seashell (memories of summers on Cape Cod)

5. postcards from New Zealand, Germany, Switzerland (to indicate a love of traveling)

6. a recipe (for cooking, a favorite pastime)

7. a published book (another Scholastic endeavor)

8. an illustration by a kindergarten child (reflecting an event from Kathy's kindergarten days)

Variations

You can also use the bags to provide insight about historical figures, book characters, cities, states, and countries.

Pages in Our Lives

Collaborate with your students on a book or a photo album about your class. A Page in the Life of… can be made in a variety of formats—from a big book with a page for each child to a photo album depicting class events and activities throughout the year. If you decide to do a page-per-child book, you may want to provide a standardized format, so that each page is like a résumé. Or some students might prefer to write an article about themselves. For example, a student might record his or her:

- name, address, phone number, and birth date
- likes and dislikes
- favorite food, books, pastimes
- a significant event
- advice for success in a certain grade
- goals for the year

Variations

Students could compile a book or photo album about their school, community, town, or state. Once completed, these could be placed in either the school or town library, donated to a senior citizen complex, or even displayed at county fairs.

All About Me From A to Z

Another way for students and teachers to learn about one another is by using the first letter of their last names to find words or phrases that describe themselves. This can be a family project that is shared at open house. Model the activity by preparing your own *All About Me From A to Z* sheet. Hang the alphabetical autobiographies in the classroom or in the hallways. When you take them down, compile them into a class book, *All About Us From A to Z*.

> Here's an introduction of "me" that I shared with 3F this week.
>
> I thought you might like to know a little about me, too.
>
> The students will be writing one of these introductions during September, also.
>
> **All About Me From A to Z**
>
> | | |
> |---|---|
> | Alice Fiske | Notices nice things |
> | Book lover | Open to new ideas |
> | Creative | Positive thinker |
> | Dreamer | Quiet inside |
> | Energetic | Reader |
> | Friend | Silly at times |
> | Gift giver | Teacher of 3rd grade |
> | Hopeful | Usually patient |
> | Innkeeper | Vermonter in the summer |
> | Junk food eater | Worrier |
> | Kindness matters | Xeroxes a lot |
> | Loves life | Young |
> | Musical | Zooming around! |

Student of the Week

Each week, feature a different student. Ask students to bring in artifacts and pictures from home to display. Have classmates interview the student of the week. Perhaps you can even grant some special privileges during the week, such as excusing the student from a day of homework or having the student have lunch with the principal. Use a body map of the child, or a generic form, to record positive things that the child's classmates volunteer about him or her. For example:

- Casey has a wonderful smile.
- She is a great artist.
- She helps me with my reading.

When the week is over, give the body map to the child to take home to share with his or her family.

We All Measure Up

This activity was inspired by the book *Measuring Penny* by Loreen Leedy. It is the story of a class assignment in which a child has to measure objects in her home using both standard and nonstandard measurements. The child chooses to measure her dog Penny in inches, centimeters, by weight, using dog bones, by how high Penny can jump, and so on. The book's charming ending says that the dog is worth a million dollars for all the pleasure and happiness it contributes to the child's life.

The unique feature of this book is the many ways the child uses measurement. Not only does this make measurement purposeful and meaningful, but it also suggests an excellent home-school activity. The children in Sue McKeighan's third-grade class made their own books, including *Measuring Izzy, Measuring Molly,* and *Measuring Paige.* Once the books were complete, they were bound with a common measuring device: a tiny ruler—a nice touch for a worthwhile math activity! If you'd like to try the activity with your class, use the reproducible on page 83. It's a fun homework follow up that involves parents in classroom learning.

Use creative binding in other ways. Punch holes through the pages of the completed book. Instead of stapling or using a binding machine, use an object that is representative of the book. A twig would be prefect for a book about the environment; a pencil is great for a book on writing or for American Education Week; a spoon could hold together a recipe book. Use a large elastic band, place the object on the cover, and then loop the elastic band around the top of the object, down the back side of the book, and finally around the bottom of the object.

Me Books

Me Books are a variation on a résumé or personal profile. Students could start their books at the beginning of the school year so that they keep growing and become a kind of mini-portfolio. If you like, use the reproducible on page 82 as a springboard for the project. In their books, students might include:

- a self-portrait

- a drawing of the student by a peer

- a photo page with snapshots of the student, his or her family, pets, home, and vacations

- a written description of the student

- fingerprints, handprints or footprints

- a general information page (name, age, address, family members, birthday, zodiac sign, interests, hobbies)

- an "ideal" page (my ideal friend, teacher, pet, vacation, day)

- a "What I would do if . . ." page (If I won a million dollars, was U.S. president for a day, was the teacher for a day, a book character, a movie star)

- a personal coat of arms

- a list of good deeds

- a "Wish Upon a Star" page (a wish for myself, family, school, country, the world)

Getting to Know You Quilt

One way to celebrate that you and your students are well on the way to getting to know one another is to construct a Getting to Know You class quilt. Give each student a quilt square on which he or she draws a self-portrait. The portrait can take up the entire space or be framed with a quiltlike border. The child places his or her name on the front of the quilt square. On the back of the square, children can write about themselves. The information can be biographical or include their goals, dreams, or words of wisdom. After each quilt square is completed, laminate it for durability and punch holes in each corner.

To form the quilt, weave the squares together with colored yarn. Cut holes in the top row so you can insert loops of yarn and hang it on a yardstick, curtain rod, or dowel. You can also construct the quilt from plastic sandwich bags. The advantage to using the plastic bags is that the contents can be easily changed and the quilt adapted to a variety of purposes.

Variation

You could also place students' pictures in the center of the quilt squares. In the four corners of the square, place information about each student.

CHAPTER THREE

The Community Rules

The word *discipline* comes from the Latin *discere*, which means "to learn." We believe that discipline means developing self-control, orderliness, and responsibility. Not only should the school address the cognitive and academic aspects of children's education, it must also help children learn to make responsible choices. A safe and orderly atmosphere is essential. After all, if a classroom is chaotic, no one can learn.

Students need to acquire internal control, to think for themselves, and to assume responsibility for both their learning and their behavior. Though you probably take care of most classroom management issues at the start of the school year, class rules need to be revisited from time to time.

Rules for Living and Learning

Just as society has to establish rules for peaceful coexistence, so do classrooms need norms for living and learning. They allow a group to work together in a peaceful, safe, efficient, and caring way.

Here's a plan. At the beginning of each school year, teachers and students sit down, brainstorm, discuss, and determine ways that their classrooms will work during that school year. A secretary—a student or one of the teachers—records the ideas, which are then reviewed over the next several days. After discussing the ideas, the group should finalize the rules and post them in the classroom where everyone can see them. Nothing is written in stone. Feel free to adjust or change the rules as needed. Developing rules collaboratively gives children a sense of ownership over what will occur in their classroom that year and contributes to the development of a sense of community.

Tips for Better Brainstorming

Here are some questions or scenarios for the class to consider.

1. What kind of a class do you think we should have this year?

2. How do you want to be treated by the other children in this school?

3. What do you think a peaceful classroom looks like?

4. What rules do you think the Pilgrims established when they first came to America? Why did they set these rules?

5. If you and a group of friends were forming a club, what rules would you want to talk about and establish?

6. Suppose we have to move to a new planet. What would we have to do to make sure everyone is treated equally and can live in peace?

Setting Up Ground Rules

This is a perfect segue for setting up ground rules. From the beginning, insist on no put-downs and give the right to pass, which means students have the option of not sharing at a particular time. If they are decided collaboratively by the class, these guidelines will be much more meaningful than if you simply impose them.

The students in Alice's third-grade class proposed these guidelines.

- Avoid bad words.
- Raise your hand or take turns.
- Listen to others.
- Make eye contact with speakers.
- Don't use insults or put-downs.
- Don't interrupt.
- Pay attention.
- Stick to the topic.
- Don't yell.
- Try to understand others' ideas.
- Don't butt in.
- Don't space out.
- Don't gossip.
- Don't horse around.
- Respect each other.
- Be responsible.
- Keep your temper.
- Work with your group.
- Learn from each other.

Now that You Have Them, What Do You Do With Class Rules?

- Post them on bulletin boards.
- Display them on charts that students create.
- Turn them into booklets.
- Copy them at the front of student notebooks.
- Send them home to parents at the start of the school year so that parents become familiar with your philosophy about discipline and learn about the procedures that will be used during the school year. Point out that the rules were developed collaboratively after much discussion.

Class Bill of Rights

Class rules can take many forms, including a bill of rights or a class constitution. Although each is obviously a great tie-in with the study of American history in the upper grades, you don't have to wait until then for children to create their own bill of rights or constitution. You do, however, need to provide some background before children can go ahead with this activity.

You might start with discussions about the rights of others and what rights we have. We have the right to learn, the right to be safe, and the right not to be disturbed, for example. If you like, you may use the reproducible on page 84 as a basis for discussion. Once you and the children decide on their rights—and, by the way, yours as well—ask for volunteers to write the document. It should be signed by all class members.

That's what Molly Oakley's fifth-grade class did. First, though, Molly had the class study the United

CLASS CONSTITUTION

We the people of Mrs. Oakley's fifth grade class, are writing this constitution in order to have peace and not chaos in our class. We will respect everybody and all property and we will cooperate with each other at all times.

We will do our best in our work and will remember our manners. We will be helpful to others. We will pay attention and listen while others are speaking. We will always acknowledge those who talk to us or who do something for us.

Inappropriate language and put-downs are forbidden. If we can't say something nice, we won't say it at all. So we will always be kind to one another and show concern for our classmates.

The whole class is the Legislative Branch of our government. The Executive Branch is made up of the class president, vice president, and the secretary. The Judicial Branch is made up of five judges who will preside over court sessions. These positions will change each month. Mrs. Oakley does have veto power and is more powerful than either the Legislative, the Executive or the Judicial Branch, though she will listen carefully to all ideas, feelings, and opinions. No student may plead the Fifth Amendment, nor have lawyers represent them in court.

We realize that the rules are constructed for the Safety, Peace, and Health of all and we sign this constitution as proof that we will follow them all year long.

Our Classroom Bill of Rights

We have a right to...
- have our own space
- tell our point of view
- have a turn to talk
- be listened to
- try new ideas
- make mistakes
- get help
- be safe
- have fun

Danielle T.	Brian	Holly
Danielle H.	Kevin	Jim
Christian	Lisa D.	Sarah W.
Christopher B.	Ashley B.	James L.
Clinton	Monica M.	Jeff
Jeremi	Brian J.	Sam B.
David	Alicia	Doug

States Bill of Rights, which she displayed in a prominent place.

She also asked her children and their families to draft or write a Family Bill of Rights. She displayed the documents in her room and in the display area right outside. Some families were creative and made their bill of rights look antiquated by tearing the edges of the paper, wrinkling, and dyeing it.

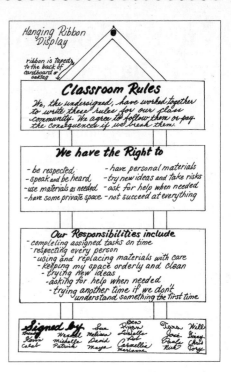

Hanging Ribbon Display

ribbon is taped to the back of cardboard or oaktag

Classroom Rules
We, the undersigned, have worked together to write these rules for our class community. We agree to follow them or pay the consequences if we break them.

We have the Right to
- be respected   - have personal materials
- speak and be heard   - try new ideas and take risks
- use materials as needed   - ask for help when needed
- have some private space   - not succeed at everything

Our Responsibilities include
- completing assigned tasks on time
- respecting every person
- using and replacing materials with care
- keeping my space orderly and clean
- trying new ideas
- asking for help when needed
- trying another time if we don't understand something the first time

Signed by

Tea-Stained Paper

MATERIALS

☆ sheets of plain white paper (copy paper works well)

☆ several tea bags

☆ two-inch-deep baking pan

STEPS

1. Tear the four edges of the paper to eliminate clean-cut edges.

2. Brew the tea bags to create a strong tea, and let it cool. The tea can be used for several days.

3. When you are ready to stain the paper, pour the tea into the pan.

4. Crumple the paper, one sheet at a time.

5. Open the sheet, dip it into the tea for a minute or so. Lay out the wet sheet on a flat surface to dry. Add darker areas by dabbing them with the soggy tea bags.

T and Y Charts

You can also create class and school rules by using T and Y charts. They get their names from their shape. T charts are for two kinds of information. Y charts allow for three categories. These charts are also really useful for setting rules about behavior in the hallway, on the playground, in gym, and on a field trip.

Suppose you do a T chart about the cafeteria, which can be chaotic and noisy. Ask children to imagine the ideal cafeteria setting; suggest that they focus on good manners and appropriate noise levels.

What does the ideal cafeteria look like?

◉ children sitting and eating quietly

◉ clean floors with no discarded paper, no dropped or spilled food

◉ kids keeping hands to themselves

◉ no one talking with their mouths full

◉ no food being thrown away

◉ receptacles filled with thrown-away items

What does the ideal cafeteria sound like?

◉ good manners (saying "please" and "thank you")

◉ inside voices

◉ no yelling

You could add a third category; then you would have a Y chart.

What does the ideal cafeteria feel like?

◉ the atmosphere is homelike

◉ the surroundings are pleasant

◉ the feeling is inviting

◉ the furnishings are comfortable

◉ people who use it and people who work there are nice to one another

◉ everyone is friendly

When two categories are used, then the T chart is the format for recording the information. Three categories use the branches of the Y to record the data.

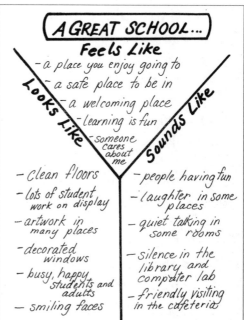

Solving Problems

Even with good intentions and all the rules in the world, even with an excellent classroom management plan, problems do arise. It's important to know that there are excellent programs that school districts can adopt to help children resolve conflicts and solve problems. They include peer-mediation programs and conflict-resolution training.

Conflict-resolution training doesn't eliminate conflict but helps children learn skills to resolve conflicts in nonviolent ways. No one way is the best. Different situations call for different resolution techniques. Conflict-resolution training helps children to recognize options that are available to them. An excellent professional resource is *Teaching Conflict Resolution Through Children's Literature* by William Kreidler.

Peer mediation is an aspect of conflict resolution that involves training children to be facilitators. If two classmates have a disagreement, for example, the facilitator can help identify the problem, discover how it makes each of the students feel, and suggest solutions. At the very least, it would take an entire book to do justice to a complete discussion of conflict resolution and peer mediation.

There are so many ways to address problems that may arise during the school year. Problems that may appear trivial, especially in the younger grades, need to be acknowledged and resolved. It's always helpful to keep an emergency kit of photos, pictures, articles, and poems that deal with conflicts (past, present, or potential) for use as discussion starters.

Community meetings are a great time to provide children with guidance in solving their problems. Here, a variety of issues may be dealt with in a supportive and caring manner. Once again, children's literature can be an effective springboard for discussion.

SOLVING PROBLEMS IN LITERATURE

NAME _____

DATE _____

Name and Description of a Character

Describe a Problem in the Story

Describe How the Character Dealt With the Problem

Explain How the Problem was Solved

Other Ways the Problem Could Have Been Handled

Venting Helps

Provide a journal in a corner of your room so children can vent and describe what is bothering them. Also leave preprinted forms for them to describe their problem and some possible solutions. Sometimes just writing about a problem is a huge help, but as is more often the case, the children want attention from their teacher. Therefore, as soon as you have some time, read what the children have written and suggested. Address the problem in a way you think most discreet and appropriate.

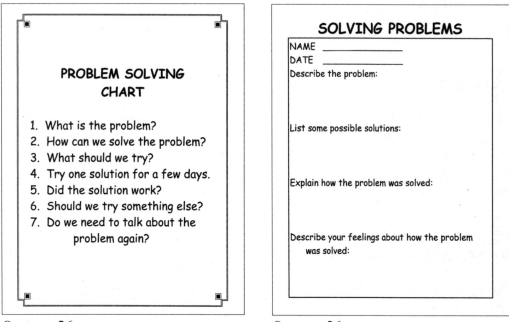

T CHART for CONFLICT	
What It Looks Like	What It Sounds Like
hitting	yelling
pushing	shouting
fighting	arguing
being mean	calling names
not sharing	insulting
biting	squabbling
people left out	swearing
mad people	teasing
kicking	fighting over
poking	things
shoving	

T CHART for SOLVING PROBLEMS	
Looks Like	Sounds Like
peer mediation	discussing
listening to each other	hearing others
cooperating	points of view
shaking hands	apologizing
negotiating	talking it out
staying away from each	saying, "I'm sorry"
other for a while	"I know how
sharing	you feel"
compromising	"Let's talk it
taking turns	over"
making peace offerings	"How can we
working together	solve this?"
getting help	

See bottom of this page.

PROBLEM SOLVING CHART

1. What is the problem?
2. How can we solve the problem?
3. What should we try?
4. Try one solution for a few days.
5. Did the solution work?
6. Should we try something else?
7. Do we need to talk about the problem again?

See page 36.

SOLVING PROBLEMS

NAME _____
DATE _____
Describe the problem:

List some possible solutions:

Explain how the problem was solved:

Describe your feelings about how the problem was solved:

See page 36.

Words of Conflict

ogether, the students can brainstorm words that deal with conflict, such as *punching, not sharing, fighting,* and *name calling.* List these on one side of a chart. On the other side, in a bright color, list the "good" equivalents. You can also create T charts that deal with the terms *conflict* and *solving problems.*

Chat to Mr. Tuttle

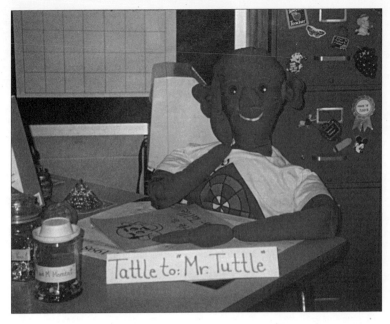

Younger children often need someone to talk to at what seems like the most inappropriate moments. Teddy Harrington, a second-grade teacher, has a helper, the adult-size Mr. Tuttle, a doll that sits at a desk in the back of her room. Next to Mr. Tuttle is a blank booklet in which children can chat with him by writing in their concerns. Mr. Tuttle is a patient listener and an amazing peacemaker—all without Teddy's help. He keeps her from having to constantly attend to the small conflicts that arise on a regular basis.

All the Room's a Stage

More active ways to deal with conflict include dramatic play, puppetry, and flannel boards. Children can act out scenarios that they create or that you give them. Props such as puppets usually work well. Children can also retell stories or make up their own using portable flannel boards. The bibliography has many stories that are well suited for this purpose.

Portable Flannel Boards

MATERIALS

☆ manila folders (folders can be laminated for durability)

☆ flannel, with adhesive on the back

☆ thickest size of interfacing (sold by crafts and sewing supply stores)

☆ crayons and markers

STEPS

1. After you laminate each folder, tape together the sides, leaving the top open.

2. Peel off the protective paper on the flannel and lay the sticky side directly onto the file folder. That's it! The flannel board is now complete.

3. Use the interfacing or flannel to make the figures for the story. Interfacing works better because it is easier to draw complete, detailed figures onto it. Once the figures are

drawn, they can be colored with crayons or markers (crayons are easier) and cut out. Store the figures in the pocket of the flannel board.

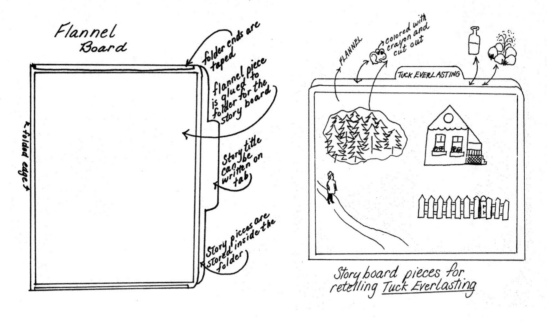

Story board pieces for retelling *Tuck Everlasting*

Student-Designed Handbooks

Rules are, of course, also needed beyond the classroom. A committee of students could design a handbook, an excellent way to promote school wide rules.

At one school, a handbook was developed by a committee of second to sixth graders who met weekly, with each meeting devoted to one aspect of school rules. After each meeting, students received minutes (written by the principal), which they shared with their classmates. Once a rule page was in draft form, it was reviewed by the entire school, and each representative was given feedback to take back to the committee. When the rules were finalized, the students themselves entered the data into a computer, and solicited and then selected illustrations from the entire school population.

The last step, before giving out booklets to the student body, was to make a presentation to the Board of Education, explaining the process and giving board members the first copies of the School Rules Handbook. This was a wonderful and positive experience for everyone—the students, the adult facilitators, and the entire school community.

This particular school had three general rules. The rules were:

1. We will be kind to ourselves and to others.

2. We will let others work and learn without being disturbed.

3. We will be responsible and accountable for everything we do.

These rules were discussed and then, accompanied by students' original illustrations, were described in meaningful and understandable terms. For example, the explanation for "We will be responsible and accountable for everything we do" became:

"This is how we do it: We clean up after ourselves. We cooperate with teachers and other students. We are honest about our behavior. When we're upset, we look for appropriate ways to express our feelings."

The booklet includes other standards as well.

We will keep school safe and clean.

We will keep school free from drugs, alcohol, tobacco, and weapons.

We will be ready and prepared for learning.

We will be honest.

We will work to the best of our ability.

We will follow the rules of our classroom.

We will dress properly for school and recess.

Then there was a listing of rules for the lunchtime cafeteria, playground, bus, and hallway.

And finally:

We will discuss these rules with other students.

Student Court

What better way for students to learn about our judicial system than to participate in it? After beginning the year with a unit on the United States Constitution, Molly Oakley and Therese Gilbert, fifth-grade teachers, have their students, in cooperative groups, brainstorm rules to govern their own classrooms. The rules have rules! Students may not preface any rule with the word *not*. No-nos include *do not interrupt* and *cannot take anyone else's belongings.* After brainstorming in groups, a spokesperson reports to the rest of the class, and the students prepare a draft of class rules, their constitution.

Introduce the concept of a student court after the rules are written. Teachers hand-pick the five members of the court to guarantee a balance. The court, which changes members monthly, has a president (who presides), a vice president, a secretary (who keeps track of punishments), and two other members. The members are sworn in on a Book of Authority.

Children have to go to court when they receive two warnings in a day; no warnings are carried over, so each day begins anew. The court may also hold emergency meetings. With the rest of the class as onlookers, the judges can receive additional input from classmates and can question the defendant. No lawyers are allowed, and students may not plead the Fifth Amendment.

Generally, the defendant is asked why he or she received warnings. If the defendant convincingly pleads innocent, the teachers can withdraw the warnings, and the case is closed. Otherwise, when the questioning is completed, the court goes into the hallway to render judgment and determine the punishment. Punishments range from loss of recess, a letter of apology to the hurt party, committing a random act of kindness (and keeping track of the act), or some other action that the court deems fair. This court system works quite well and allows the students to practice self-evaluation and self-discipline.

Think Positively

An important part of learning is taking on challenges and making mistakes. Children need to realize that mistakes are normal parts of the learning process and that they are more acceptable if the students think positively.

To help students focus on the positive, brainstorm words that convey good feelings, such as *kindness, cooperation, respect, trustworthiness, teamwork,* and *honesty*. Then, use the reproducible on page 85 to stimulate a class discussion. When you discuss negative feelings, perhaps after reading *Feelings* by Aliki, suggest that students provide positive ways of coping with the negative feelings. For example:

CHAPTER 3: Think Positively

WE ALL MAKE CHOICES

A Winner will say...	A Loser will say...
I'll try.	no.
let's do it.	I don't want to.
I'm getting better.	I'm terrible at this.
maybe there's another way.	this doesn't work.
let's ask for help	I quit.
give someone else a turn.	I had it first.
you can join us.	there's no room.
that was a good try.	it stinks.

WINNERS AND LOSERS

A Winner...	A Loser...
uses time wisely.	wastes time.
tries harder.	quits easily.
helps others.	refuses to help others.
gives compliments.	uses put downs.
focuses on the positive.	focuses on the negative.
admits mistakes.	blames others.
is dependable.	can't be depended on.
succeeds.	fails.
shows appreciation.	ignores others' contributions.
puts forth best effort.	doesn't try.

Teaching Kids to Care & Cooperate Scholastic Professional Books — 85

10 Ways of Coping with Anger/Frustration

1. Leave the room.
2. Count to ten.
3. Play some soothing music.
4. Write in a journal.
5. Talk to someone.
6. Start over.
7. Ask for help.
8. Go slower.
9. Take a break.
10. Choose something else to do.

Pillowcase Quilt

A pillowcase quilt can depict a harmonious, safe, and productive classroom or school. On individual squares of fabric, children illustrate some aspect of what makes their class or school special. Display the finished product in the classroom, hallways, school library, or in the school's district office for all to enjoy.

A Pillowcase Quilt

MATERIALS

- ☆ pillowcase
- ☆ batting
- ☆ needle and thread
- ☆ optional iron-on fabric
- ☆ fabric markers, permanent ink pens, fabric swatches
- ☆ rod for hanging quilt

STEPS

1. Fold and press the case into thirds widthwise, then into quarters lengthwise. Use the hem for the title at the top or the bottom of the quilt.

2. Cut the batting to size and place it inside the case, smoothing it with your hand.

3. Machine or hand-stitch the folded creases to create the squares. Students can draw directly onto the case or on another piece of fabric, which can be ironed or sewn on.

4. If you use iron-on fabric, sandwich it between the pillowcase and fabric; with the heat application, bind the two pieces of material together.

5. Students can now add their illustrations.

6. Cut a small slit into each end of the top of the case and insert a hanging rod.

CHAPTER FOUR

Accentuate the Positive

Recognizing the individual contributions of your students is an important part of building a caring class. Recognition can be as basic as spending part of community meetings mentioning kids' achievements and accomplishments. It can be as elaborate as a special school assembly.

Good News Notes

Some schools implement Catch Someone Doing Something Good programs. Anyone doing something positive for the class or school receives a good news or good word note. The notes, which you can print on ready-made forms, can be presented without fanfare, or they can be featured on a bulletin board outside the principal's office. The bulletin board display might include the recipients' photos and a description of their deeds. After a week or two, send both home to the children's parents.

Alice looks for a positive contribution from each child in her class. Sometimes she acknowledges excellence or improvement in schoolwork—knowing the times tables, for example, or proficiency in cursive writing. Sometimes she rewards those who helped without being asked, those who handled a tough situation, and so on. She presents a certificate every other week until every child in her class has received one.

Others in your school should also be encouraged to reward students with good news notes. For example, in one of Alice's weekly newsletters to parents, she included a column entitled Comments From Other Teachers and Friends. Before they took home the newsletter, she challenged her students to find others who could write something positive about their week.

Happy Thoughts

C hildren can also take responsibility for recognizing their classmates' accomplishments. Introduce a happy-thoughts jar filled with children's eyewitness accounts of good deeds done by their classmates. You don't have to use a jar; any container works well, but it will be most effective if it is clear enough for the contents to be seen.

When you introduce the happy-thoughts jar, read aloud excerpts from *Donovan's Word Jar,* a book by Monalisa deGross. Donovan collects words in a jar. He ends up with so many interesting words that he doesn't have room for them all. He decides to give away his extra words to people those words describe or those to whom the words would be meaningful.

Students could write and present positive words to their classmates, a nice way to recognize special times and attributes.

During your daily wrap-up meeting at the end of the day, read aloud the contributions in the jar. This meeting is a time when the class reviews and reflects on the day, and discusses issues that may have cropped up since the morning community meeting. You or a student can read the slips aloud. Usually, the number of slips is manageable enough for all to be read in one sitting.

Variations

Have a penny-for-your-thoughts jar. Collect pennies and place them in a container. At the school year's end, donate them to a cause chosen by the class—to the family of a hospitalized student, for example, to a homeless shelter, or to an environmental protection group.

Send Home Newsletters

N ewsletters are another way to recognize and compliment members of the school community, whether they are students or staff. Most schools send home a monthly newsletter and many teachers write a weekly bulletin. These make excellent forums for recognizing students, class volunteers, and guest speakers. They are also effective ways to showcase student writing

and artwork. The writing can be the product of regular class work or articles done specifically for your publication. Ask for student volunteers to interview new teachers, new students, guest speakers, and artists in residence.

Tie in compliments or positive thoughts with study units. When her class was studying *Charlotte's Web*, one of our colleagues did a web activity called Some Kid! She asked her students to place their own names in a designated spot on a web and to think of some compliments Charlotte might have written about them. After the compliments were recorded, children displayed their webs in the classroom. The webs served as daily reminders of their positive thoughts and attributes.

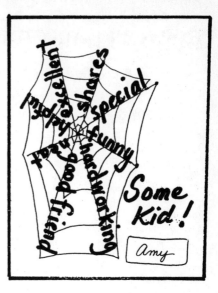

A Marble for Your Thoughts

Give students the chance to evaluate themselves. Many of our colleagues love the idea of the marble jar. This time, fill the jar with marbles for good deeds, good behavior, and so on. During the first week of school, demonstrate how the class can recognize good behavior and the appropriate way to reward it. After that, the children can evaluate themselves. At the end of each day, during the wrap-up meeting, the children must agree on how many marbles they should receive that day, and why they should receive them. This activity helps children get into the habit of group discussion and self-evaluation.

Once the jar is full, ask students for ideas on the kind of rewards they have earned. Alice gives each student a sheet of paper and asks him or her to list three appropriate suggestions. She eliminates duplicates and places the remaining ones on a ballot. The students then vote for their reward.

The rewards have included watching a video, having a special snack, and receiving free time. (One full jar equals one hour of free time.) Occasionally, students

bank their free time until they have accumulated even more. Sometimes you should choose the reward (with student approval), which becomes an incentive for filling the jar. Generally, this reward is something that the students have expressed an interest in, such as a popular book.

The size of the jar and the number of students influence how frequently the jar is filled. In Alice's class, the jar tends to be filled once a month or once every six weeks.

Showcase Accomplishments

Set aside a space in the school for recognizing students' accomplishments, much the way middle schools and high schools display trophies in showcases. In the space, you could spotlight:

- a student or citizen of the month (one from each classroom)
- Presidential Fitness Award winners
- academic achievers and those on the honor roll
- all-county music participants
- participants in class plays and production photos
- photographs of students studying
- special classroom/school events
- good news about the school
- a teacher, administrator, or paraprofessional
- guest speakers and other visitors
- class projects
- student artwork

For student art work, feature one grade each month. The work can be individual works or whole-class projects, such as an ocean mural. At the end of the year, hold an art show focusing on what each class did in art class.

Set Goals

Jack Mulholland, a principal, has the children in his school set personal yearly goals. He meets with each child for a demonstration of how that goal has been met. Each child's name is then placed on a scroll outside the main office. Some goals that students have chosen include excellence in cursive writing, reading a novel and discussing it, and memorizing the multiplication tables.

Remember that not only students deserve recognition. You can honor community members, retirees, and school workers, such as bus drivers, custodians, cafeteria workers, school nurses, and secretaries. The school calendar is filled with special recognition days for school workers. These include secretaries (April), nurses (January), teachers (May), and

Teacher Appreciation Book

The best thing about my teacher is...
- she plays music in class
- she reads us great books
- she smiles when I come in
- she plays the piano
- she has a soft voice
- she likes kids!

I like it when my teacher is...
- laughs
- does science experiments
- lunch with our class
- extra chapters
- outside to draw for fun
- homework

Appreciation Books

Our School Secretary has so many jobs, she...
- answers the phone
- take messages
- says nice things to visitors
- tells people where rooms are
- calls the buses
- helps the Principal
- runs the school

sample from Secretary Appreciation Book

What is a School Nurse?
She is someone who...
- takes care of you when your Mom can't
- gives us bandaids
- cleans up after we throw up
- calls our home if we have a fever
- is a friend to us

sample from School Nurse Appreciation Book

retirees (June). Devote a section in your newsletter to people being honored, with the students contributing messages, poems, articles, advice, and illustrations. Write class letters to workers thanking them for their contributions.

Budding Journalists

Don't forget your local newspapers! They serve the school community and probably appreciate publishing information that recognizes students. In addition to the usual publication of honor rolls, pictures of students of the month, and special events, some newspapers also welcome articles by students. For instance, students in one school participate in a Silhouette program, during which they spend time with a variety of workers in the community as a way to explore different careers and strengthen school-community ties. The children who take part write the newspaper article that appears along with a photograph.

One of our favorite student-written articles in a local weekly newspaper was about a mother-daughter presentation during a school assembly. They spoke about their visit to Antarctica. Carole Lewis was the lucky fourth grader who experienced the adventurous field trip. If you like, use Carole's report on page 86 to invite students to share their own adventures in a narrative form.

Book It

If your schools wants to honor the accomplishments of its staff in more unique ways, consider creating personalized books. Possible titles that will make someone very happy are: *The Best (Nicest) Thing About My Teacher…*, *What Is a Secretary?*, and *Our Nurse Kathy Corbin Calls the Shots.*

Throw Bouquets

Giving cut flowers (that don't last very long) may be a traditional gesture of thanks, but imagine students making long-lasting bouquets of paper and straws. Design individual flower petals attached to stems

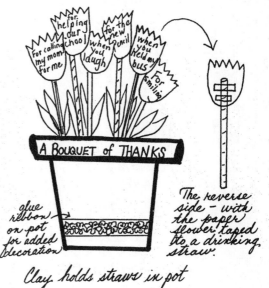

glue ribbon on pot for added decoration

A BOUQUET of THANKS

The reverse side – with the paper flower taped to a drinking straw.

Clay holds straws in pot

made of straws, and place them in clay pots. Cover the flower pots with fabric or attach a bow and present it to the recipient with a card saying, "Here's A Bouquet of Thanks!"

Good-Deed Book

Place a good-deed book in your class library. At first, this book will just be a cover with blank pages. But, like the happy-thoughts jar, it will get more and more use, for this is yet another chance for students to describe someone's good deeds. A photograph, an illustration, or a reflection on how the good deed affected the entry's writer should accompany each inscription. The good deeds don't have to be limited to the classroom; add good deeds that were reported by newspapers about your community, state, or even the world.

Thank-You Quilt

This is an excellent way to recognize the contributions of school personnel. Construct a framed quilt. On slips of paper, write the names of the people whom you want to honor in your school. Each student draws a name and makes a quilt square for that person. Because the quilt square will be done from a student's perspective, he or she will have to interview the subject to find out pertinent biographical information. Place this information on the four sides of a picture frame. Inside the frame, place a portrait or photo. Present the quilt to the person and display it so the entire school community can share and admire it.

A Folded Frame

1. Begin with a square piece of paper. Mark the midpoints of the four sides.

2. Fold each corner to the center point using the marked midpoints as a guide for each fold.

3. Then fold each point under until it reaches the inner edge fold.

4. The finished frame can be glued in place after a photo or drawing is in place.

A Frame Quilt made of folded paper frames glued to wallpaper!

Variations

Make a quilt that recognizes the contributions of people who have made a difference (Women's History Month in March); poets (Poetry Month in April); African Americans (Black History Month in February); peacemakers, environmentalists, authors (Children's Book Week in April); and so on.

CHAPTER FIVE

Ripples of Kindness

I n many classrooms, the exchange of information tends to go mainly in one direction—from the teacher to the student. However, in a caring, responsive classroom, learning can flow in both directions as teachers and students work together to achieve high standards and respect for one another.

Kindness Matters

K indness is contagious and, in fact, has a ripple effect that will reach beyond the school's doors and into the children's homes and communities. Kindness can be the theme of a unit on Martin Luther King Jr. and the nonviolence movement that he led. Ask students to read King's writings and discuss the dreams he had for humankind.

Read with the class the "I Have a Dream" speech that Dr. King delivered in Washington, D.C., in 1963, then encourage the children to write their own versions of it. Decorate classrooms and school hallways with illustrations of their dreams for a peaceful society. Recently, Dr. King's son initiated a program honoring his late father—the Do Something: Kindness and Justice Challenge. For this challenge, participating students, schools, and student organizations perform individual acts of kindness and justice (KJ) while learning important values such as respect, responsibility, tolerance, compassion, generosity, and moral courage. The acts of kindness and justice can be posted on the KJ Web site (www.dosomething.org), a way to share stories and experiences with other participants. If you like, request a KJ Challenge Educator Guide; it contains everything you need to implement the program. Log on to the site for more information.

After completing the unit about Dr. King's contributions to the civil rights and peace movements, share excerpts from the *Random Acts of Kindness* books published by Conari Press.

Random Acts of Kindness Week (RAK) occurs annually during the week of

Valentine's Day in February. During that time, schools across the country plan special activities and events and join in with community organizations for local celebrations.

Random acts of kindness are those sweet or lovely things that people do for no apparent reason except to help someone else. The acts can be as spontaneous as sharing a lunch, putting good news notes on someone's desk, or picking up litter on the school grounds. Or they can be more involved—collecting food, clothing, or money for a homeless shelter, for example, or conducting button campaigns to spread the news about kindness.

Kindness Journals

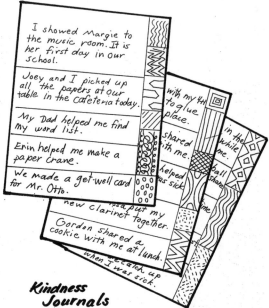

Creating Acts of Kindness journals can become a daily activity leading up to Random Acts of Kindness Week. Students record what they do for others, what random act of kindness someone has done for them, or an event they may have witnessed. Ask each class member to choose one of his or her entries to share during the end-of-the-day meeting.

Kindness Journals

The Thoughtful Box

Teddy Harrington's second-grade class acknowledges kindness and thoughtfulness throughout the year by using a Thoughtful Box. This decorated box is placed in a strategic place in the classroom, along with slips of paper. When students observe something nice or when someone does something thoughtful for them, they write about it and place it in the box. All the responses are shared and applauded during a community meeting at the end of the week.

Kindness Learning Center

While you're using the kindness theme, students can participate in an Acts of Kindness Learning Center. Some Learning Center activities are:

- Read and respond to books about kindness in a variety of ways, such as through art, writing, and crafts.

- Make friendship circles.

- Draw cartoons depicting characters who are cooperating or helping someone.

⊙ Fill in an organizer that lists ways the student is like one of his or her classmates and how he or she is different.

⊙ Complete a chart titled Friends Care About One Another. Children tell who the friend is, how they demonstrate caring about that friend, and why they care about the friend.

⊙ Read and write instructions on how to be a good friend, a kind person, and care for someone else. Place these instructions in a class book to go in the class library.

⊙ Create bumper-sticker slogans with thoughts about kindness.

⊙ Make friendship bookmarks.

Friendship Circles

MATERIALS

☆ paper plate or paper circle, one for each child

☆ writing utensils

STEPS (for students)

Friendship Circle

1. Divide the plate or circle into four pie-shaped pieces.

2. Each student should place a photograph or illustration of himself or herself in the center and label it with his or her name.

3. In each of the four sections, write the names of four friends, along with a picture and/or description of each.

4. As part of the description, tell how that friend has helped the student, or how the student has helped the friend.

Variation

Each student can describe four acts of kindness or friendship that he or she has done recently for someone else, for the school, or for the community.

Using Technology

This year, during Alice's Acts of Kindness unit, her students used their technology skills to design business cards. They also made bookmarks with mottos pertaining to both kindness and quilting. Some of the mottos were: Piece Together a Kind World; Piece by Piece, We'll Build a Better World; and Everybody's Piece Counts. The students even designed placards urging Practice Acts of Kindness and held a peaceful demonstration at the school.

Countdown to RAK Week

Each day, share one or two ways that kindness can be practiced. Ask students to write them up in brief announcements that can be read over the public address system.

Students can also choose a word that symbolizes this effort, such as *love, kindness, peace, caring,* and *sharing* to make a big-letter design. Display the word at the Peace Tea (see below) and take good care of it so it can be used for years to come as a memento of that particular class. This is a real community builder in Alice's classes, as each year her students choose a different word. Next to the work, place a sign that credits the students who chose and designed the word. This is a way to create a feeling of continuity from one class to the next. Alice has found that former students like to visit and reminisce about their year in that classroom.

Winding Down on a High Note

The culmination of the unit can occur during the official Random Acts of Kindness Week in February. There are many activities that can be used for the closing celebration, including schoolwide assemblies, publishing the students' efforts in an Acts of Kindness magazine or newspaper, or inviting others to a classroom party or tea. Alice's class hosts a Peace Tea each year, inviting parents and some community members. The previous year's class is always invited to be present at the dress rehearsal. During the Peace Tea, the children recite poetry and sing songs that have been part of their community meetings. The students then serve their guests tea and cookies, again an opportunity for addressing proper etiquette and behavior. In keeping with the community philosophy, reflection is important, and throughout the experience the children gather and discuss the activities and their feelings, as well as reveal their thoughts in writing. If you like, use the reproducible on page 87 to help students organize their thoughts and feelings about the Peace Tea.

Kindness Activities

Here are more activities for your Acts of Kindness celebration. They would, in fact, be effective at any time.

- Invite the principal, teachers, and students to start each day with a reading about kindness.

- Create a kindness quilt to display at school, at the district office, the office of a local government official, or the town library.

- Collect items for food shelters or for the homeless.

- Create murals that depict kindness; donate them to nursing homes or senior citizen centers.

- List words, phrases, or quotations that describe kindness.

- Create a Happy Time file of sayings, cartoons, and pictures to give to someone who needs a smile.

- Locate articles or pictures in newspapers or magazines that are about kindness.

- Place a daily kindness quote on your bulletin board or on chart paper.

- Leave words of kindness for school workers, such as the secretaries, school nurse, and aides.

- Divide a piece of paper into four sections (Me, My Town, My State, My Country) and record ideas for kindness in each.

- Visit a retirement community or a nursing home and spend time with those who request the company of children.

- Pick up litter on the school grounds.

- Write positive notes to classmates or other people in your school.

- Make a kindness collage of pictures and words found in magazines.

- Write Acts of Kindness on footprint shapes and place them on a wall in the school with the title "Follow the way to a better school and a better world."

Thoughts About Peace Tea
by _____

Today we will videotape our performance. How do you feel about that?

_____
_____

What is your favorite part of our performance (not counting refreshments)?

_____
_____

What part of our performance do we do the BEST?

_____
_____

What do you think is the audience's favorite part?

_____
_____

How do you think the _____ graders will feel coming back to this class to see the performance today?

_____
_____

How do you feel about performing for the _____ graders?

_____
_____

Why? _____
_____

You Can Make a Difference

The newspaper *USA TODAY* created Make a Difference Day to celebrate and reward the efforts of Americans. And its news stories highlight many of the Make a Difference efforts made by people across the nation. Share these stories with your students as examples of how people of all ages can make a difference.

Make a difference! For instance, one of our schools has a yearly project of collecting funds for needy families during holiday time. This is part of a wider scheme that benefits many families and provides clothing and food. In addition, each faculty member at that school draws the name of a child and gifts him or her with an educational toy and a book.

Each student writes their name and draws a hand on the blank library pocket or an envelope. The pockets are posted on a display board. Students are encouraged to write a note if someone helps them or if they observe others helping.

Lend a Hand

Use library-card pockets to construct a bulletin board with a Lend a Hand theme. Students trace their hands on the pockets or draw them if their hands are too large, and write their names nearby. Decorate the hands and fingers, and personalize them with fabric, lace trim, nail polish, glitter, and so on. Attach the pockets to poster board or your bulletin board with the title Lend a Hand. As each child witnesses or experiences a good deed or a helping hand, he or she writes a note about the gesture and places it inside that child's pocket.

Friends Always

What does friendship mean? Some lovely books about friendship are appropriate for all levels. They include *Frog and Toad Are Friends*, *Let's Be Enemies*, and *Some Friend*. After your book session, talk about the qualities that contribute to a friendship. Ask students to keep these five essential questions in mind.

- ◉ What does friendship mean?
- ◉ What keeps friends together?
- ◉ What kinds of problems can hurt a friendship?
- ◉ What are good things about having a friend?
- ◉ What is the most important thing about being a friend?

Accentuate the Negative?

For another point of view, *How to Lose All Your Friends,* by Nancy Carlson, provides "advice" on what to do if you don't want to have any friends. Never smile. Never share. Be a bully. Be a poor sport. Tattle. Whine. Share some lighter moments as your students add to this list.

Six Friendly Things to Do

1. Languages and Hugs

At your morning meeting, talk about the importance of language and gestures to friendship. What kinds of words help us make and keep friends? Talk about the greetings friends use, words of parting, and the role of smiles, handshakes, gestures, body language, hugs, and pats on the back.

2. Pocketful of Friendship

Design a fabric (denim works beautifully) or construction-paper pocket and attach it to poster board or a thin piece of wood. Give the pocket activity a title, such as A Pocketful of Friendship or A Friendship Pocket. Ask children to each write on index cards one quality that makes a good friend and place

them in the pocket. The children could also write the name of a book character who is a good friend and explain why they chose him or her. This friendship pocket could become a learning center, with the contents being read during center time, placed in the class library, or shared occasionally during community meeting time.

3. Friendship Tree

This activity encourages and recognizes acts of friendship. Place a tree branch in a coffee container and weigh it down with sand so it won't tip over. You can also use a paper branch on a bulletin board, which may make a steadier substitute. On the branch, hang cards with messages about acts of friendship. A variation would be to hang book shapes on the tree that list books about friendship. A brief annotation can be placed on the back "cover" of the book.

4. Wanted: A Good Friend

Create posters or ads that describe characteristics of a good friend. Characters from books could be used in this activity, such as Charlotte in *Charlotte's Web* or Jess and Leslie in *Bridge to Terabithia*. Be sure to include reasons why this person is a good friend.

> Friend Wanted:
> Someone about 9 years old who enjoys soccer. Is a good sport. Is honest and helpful. Likes to ride bikes.
> Contact Tracey

Newspaper WANT AD: Classroom Community

5. The Friendship Box

For one or two weeks, class members can keep track of all the friendly things that they do for one another. These things are written on a note and put in the Friendship Box. The box can be a decorated shoe box, a colorful tissue box, or any other suitable container. Before the end of the school day, share and discuss the notes. What a friendly way to say good-bye for the day!

> WANTED: A FRIEND
> Someone who is clever and caring. A good speller. Never gives up. Likes barns.

Newspaper WANT AD: Book Character (Charlotte)

6. Picture This: Friendly Messages

Tape students' photos on a piece of paper, leaving plenty of room for written comments beneath the photograph. The photos are passed around the room, with each student adding a positive comment. The process is continued until the paper is completed. After the pictured person has had the opportunity to enjoy what his/her classmates have written, the pictures can be placed in a class photo album.

Kind Deeds Quilt

Give each child a quilting square with a heart in the center. In the four corners of the block, leave spaces for the students to record kind deeds. Make a quilt featuring kind deeds highlighting acts of kindness for which children had to extend themselves. Some examples: "I lent Justin the *I Spy* book, even though I really wanted to use it." "I saw somebody spill a box of paper clips in the hallway, and there must have been 10,000 of them, but I stayed until they were all picked up."

Plastic-Bag Quilt

MATERIALS

☆ quart or gallon self-closing plastic bags

☆ clear packing tape or colored tape

☆ one small piece of cardboard for each bag

☆ string or ribbon

☆ yardstick

STEPS

1. On a large, flat surface, such as the floor or a table, place the desired number of bags side by side in rows, each bag touching its neighbor.

2. Tape the bags together, both vertically and horizontally. To help keep the bags from moving, place the cardboard inside each. The cardboard can be retained for durability as well when the students' work is inserted inside.

3. To hang the quilt, attach string or ribbon onto the corner of each bag. Loop the ribbon and tape both ends. Make the loop large enough to insert a yardstick, so the quilt can be hung on hooks anywhere in the classroom.

CHAPTER SIX

Beyond the Classroom

I am writing this letter to ask for your help.
Do you know who I am?
I am the planet, Earth.
But I am more than just a planet.
I am your Home. I am your Mother Earth.
And just like you, there is only one of me,
so I am very special.
I need to be loved and cared for, just like you.
                    —Schim Schimmel

These powerful words, from *Dear Children of the Earth: A Letter from Home* by Schim Schimmel, set the tone for this chapter. If we are all to be connected, we must extend this connection beyond our own small community and into the larger world. Poetry is perfect for introducing a unit on the environment. An excellent collection for this purpose is *The Earth Is Painted Green: A Garden of Poems About Our Planet* by Barbara Brenner. Her poems depict "the magic and power of Earth's green things" and are a tribute to nature.

After reading the poems, children can collect others like them for a class anthology. In the upper grades, assign a committee of students to collect credits for each of the books, much like the bibliography at the end of this one. List the copyright holder of each poem at the end of your book.

As part of your Earth Day celebration, present your collection to the school library. Every morning, students and teachers can take turns reading appropriate poems over the public-address system. Post the poems throughout the school to heighten environmental awareness. Poems about Earth can also serve as springboards for students' own writing; these can be collected, bound, placed in newsletters, and submitted to publications that publish children's writing.

Bulletin Board

Make Caring for the Earth the theme of a bulletin board, which could be an ongoing and ever-growing tribute to our planet. In the center of the bulletin board, place a model of Earth surrounded by the students' hands or by figures representing children around the world. On the bulletin board place such items as:

- poems about the environment (written by the children or by published authors)
- articles in magazines or newspapers about environmental issues, such as pollution, warming trends, endangered species, and measures to preserve nature
- illustrations of environmental concerns
- maps depicting rain forests, migration patterns of endangered butterflies or birds, and locations of endangered species
- student-written reviews of books about caring for the environment
- recycling tips

What Would Our World Be Like?

The study of endangered species fascinates children, but many do not realize the impact that the loss of such animals would have on our planet. Introduce this aspect by challenging students (and yourself) to find pictures in magazines, newspapers, and books of endangered animals. Ask: What do these animals have in common? Follow with a discussion of what our world would be like without the animals, the reasons for their disappearance, and possible solutions to the problem.

Children could create books containing their research about endangered animals, such as the Envelope Books described in the following how-to. Then,

Teaching Kids to Care & Cooperate Scholastic Professional Books

older children could go to the classrooms of younger children and read what they have written (or vice versa). Students could share their creations on visits to nursing homes or senior citizen complexes, and some contributions could be published in class or school publications.

Envelope Books

MATERIALS

☆ 6" x 9" mailing envelopes or letter-size envelopes

STEPS

1. Slit the tops of the envelopes or leave them intact so that they can be folded over and attached with the clasp.

2. Paste pictures of or draw the endangered species on the front of the envelope.

3. Inside, place information about an animal, a map of where it can be located, reasons why it is endangered, ways that it is being protected, and other pictures.

4. Punch holes along the side of the envelopes so they can be attached with yarn or metal rings. This book has the advantage of being able to expand when new information is obtained or when other endangered species are added.

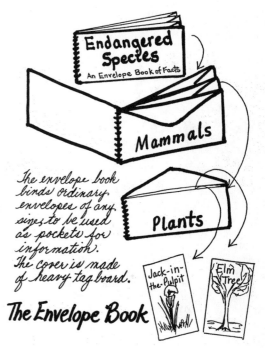

The envelope book binds ordinary envelopes of any sizes to be used as pockets for information. The cover is made of heavy tagboard.

The Envelope Book

The Earth at Our Fingertips: Pollution

It may be hard for people living in urban areas to imagine what life is like without tall buildings, concrete, and noisy cars. In other, more rural areas, it may be difficult to imagine what life surrounded by skyscrapers, traffic, and limited playing space is like. Books, virtual field trips on the Internet, magazine articles, and so on can take children to other environments so that they can gain a wider perspective of environmental issues. "Visiting" other areas and discussing environmental concerns can be an eye-opening experience.

Pollution affects every area, urban and rural alike. Suggest that children brainstorm the ways different areas might suffer from pollution. Remember that cities have trees and open green areas, while rural places may house office complexes and manufacturing plants.

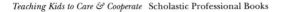

Looking Out

Use a wordless book, *The Window* by Jeanie Baker, to illustrate the effects of human encroachment on nature. The book begins with a mother and her child looking out a window at a pristine rural setting. As the child grows, the setting outside the window also changes; as it becomes more populated, it becomes increasingly polluted. The book does end on a positive note, though, with the view from the window beginning to improve from attempts to clean up the environment.

Children could create their own window scenes, perhaps choosing other settings around the world, such as a rain forest, the moon, or a river. The children could then create a box book to house scenes depicting changes that are occurring, for better and for worse. To do this activity, you could also use photographs. You might call the box book *What I See Through My Window*.

Box Books

MATERIALS

☆ boxes with plastic covers, such as those that hold greeting cards, baby items, or baked goods, to use as covers for books

☆ pieces of paper cut to fit the dimensions of the box, for use as pages

☆ small pieces of cloth

☆ crayons or markers

☆ thin colored tape

STEPS

1. The boxes usually have some depth, so the book can contain many individual pages, as well as a title page that lists the title of the book; the student author; and, if the book is adapted from a published book, its author and publisher.

2. Decorate the box to resemble an actual window by attaching cloth along its sides and top to serve as curtains; drawing lines on the plastic; or using tape to make windowpanes.

3. As its subject, the book can take an unpolluted environment and trace its route to pollution, or conversely, take a polluted environment and show the steps being taken to clean it.

4. Readers access the book by removing the plastic top and looking at the individual pages.

A Box Book

Variations

Other books can also be springboards for discussion or extension activities dealing with pollution. For example, read *The Wump World* by Bill Peet and *The Lorax* by Dr. Seuss. Compare and contrast these two books by using a Venn diagram. The books can also lead to a discussion of ways to help the environments in their stories.

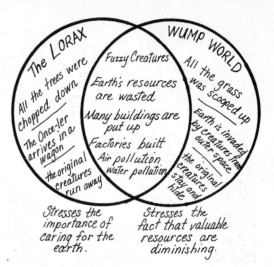

Environmental Education

Environmental education should be a lifelong process that begins in the early grades and instills lasting habits for the future caretakers of Earth. By introducing children to environmental education, you are laying a foundation of skills and knowledge that will help children make good decisions for the future of Earth.

To preserve our planet, each of us must be aware of ways we can keep it clean and healthy. We can affect the environment in ways both good and bad. In the classroom, you can explore the positive and negative aspects. Topics to discuss and research could include:

- renewable natural resources, such as trees, and nonrenewable ones, such as metals and oil
- products that contribute to waste
- biodegradable and nonbiodegradable waste
- human use of natural resources
- recycling
- how technology can improve the environment
- product packaging
- garbage

It is beyond the scope of this book to do justice to an all-inclusive unit on environmental education. However, we'd like to suggest some activities that are examples of what you and your students can do. Keep in mind that businesses, industry groups, and government agencies have developed resource kits, pamphlets, and data sheets that can be of value. For example, you can find *Aluminum Beverage Cans: The ABCs of Environmental Education*, distributed by the Can Manufacturers' Institute, at www.cancentral.com/canc/abc.htm.

Packaging for Eternity?

Did you know that in one year a class of 25 students can generate packaging waste that weighs between six and eight tons, as much as a bull elephant? (That fact is courtesy of the Can Institute.) In 1995 the U.S. Environmental Protection Agency estimated that the average person generates about 550 pounds of container and packaging waste every year.

Looking at product packaging can provide valuable insights into ways consumers and businesses affect the environment. Objectives for learning about the packaging of products include raising awareness of how packaging uses resources and how it can be natural, manufactured, or made from recycled materials. Five key questions and considerations are:

1. What are the aims of packaging?

2. Is packaging always necessary?

3. What kinds of resources are used to create packaging?

4. Are those resources renewable?

5. Can those resources be recovered through reuse or recycling?

To begin an investigation into packaging, ask students to bring in examples they have around the house. Display them in an Environmental Center. The samples could include: CD boxes; glass jars; plastic bottles; aluminum cans; cereal boxes; candy wrappers; cookie or cracker boxes; foam containers; shrink-wrapping for fruits and vegetables; cardboard containers; natural packages, such as peanut shells, bananas, orange skins, and eggshells; and packaging made of recycled products.

Ask students to:

◎ classify the types of packages

◎ discuss the economic vs. environmental issues concerning packaging

◎ research the implications of the amount of waste that results from packaging

◎ find ways that this waste can be minimized

◎ think of new use for household items using the reproducible on page 88

So where does trash go? Extend your initial investigation into a general study of trash and garbage, as well as ways the children can contribute to protecting Earth by reusing and recycling.

Environmental Word Walls

Next to the Environmental Center—as part of the bulletin board on Caring for the Earth bulletin board, for example, display key vocabulary words pertaining to the environment. Some of the words that could be displayed include:

biodegradable   recycling

landfill   acid rain

packaging   compost

nonbiodegradable

renewable resources

WORD WALL

biodegradable | acid rain | recycle
compost | renewable resource
Pollution | ozone layer | landfill

Building Our Vocabulary
CARING for EARTH

This word wall was made by taping 3×5 index cards to a wall in the classroom. When the unit is complete the cards are put in an index file for future reference.

12 Ways to Extend Your Study

1. Visit recycling centers.

2. Collect recycled products.

3. Investigate school environmental uses/abuses, such as how much plastic is used in the cafeteria, how much paper is wasted in classrooms, and so on.

4. Ask students to write to your principal, commenting on the amount of plastic utensils used in the school cafeteria.

5. Contribute to a Heal the Earth class book, an ongoing book in which students place their suggestions for a healthy Earth.

6. Think of new uses for common products.

7. Collect and display recycled products.

8. Prepare a newspaper on environmental issues.

9. Write poems, stories, and articles about the environment.

10. Read two major environmental facts over the public-address system every morning.

11. Organize a school or community yard sale to encourage reusing games, books, and toys.

12. Create a bulletin board for showcasing what the class has done to help improve the environment. You could call it We've Made a Difference.

Heal
the Earth
an ongoing class book...

Don't let the water run too long—it is wasteful.

Recycle ALL papers.

Things We've Done to Make a Difference...

LOCAL NEWS
4th Graders CLEAN Local Park

We organized a parade for Earth Day

We wrote letters to packing companies
TUNA *dolphin safe

We put up a birdfeeder outside our window

NO MORE STYROFOAM in our cafeteria

Our school planted 25 trees.

PAPER
We all recycle!

Earth Day Journals

Throughout your Earth Day study, ask students to keep journals in which they can reflect on what they've learned and experienced. Students could also:

- record thoughts and feelings about articles they've read in newspapers
- create bumper stickers or slogans with environmental messages
- keep track of what goes into the class wastepaper basket
- find Earth-smart cleaners
- prepare lists of recycled products
- describe ways to recycle at home
- design a plan to clean up the stream in your hometown

Some prompts you might use for journal writing include:

- The custodians complain that students throw their papers and food on the floor and in the hallways. List (or discuss) some ways to stop this practice.
- Pretend you are Mother Earth. Write a letter suggesting ways that people could care for the Earth.
- Pretend you are an endangered species. Write a letter telling how you could be saved.
- Why is it important to recycle? What are some ways to recycle?

CHAPTER SEVEN

Caring for Other People

Compassion, empathy, and thoughtfulness are the foundations of a caring community. Again, literature is a perfect lead-in to a discussion. *Wilfred Gordon McDonald Partridge* by Mem Fox is the story of a boy with four names, who befriends people living in community housing for the elderly.

After they read how Wilfred Gordon McDonald Partridge helps Miss Nancy, one of the residents, children can brainstorm ways that they too can be helpful. Here are some actions they might take.

- Adopt an elderly neighbor and remember that person throughout the year with notes, cards, phone calls, and visits.
- Deliver handwritten notes to children in local hospitals.
- Collect books, toys, or clothing to give to groups that can distribute them to less fortunate children.
- Record songs to share with people who are shut in.
- Send thank-you notes to people who have made a difference in your school and community.
- Collect coins to contribute to a worthy cause.
- Write and mail letters to people in the armed forces serving overseas.

Peaceful Moments

Help children learn how to take responsibility for the world beyond their immediate surroundings. Encourage them to behave in the following ways.

- Treat others as they would like to be treated.
- Accept everyone.
- Work cooperatively with everyone.

⊚ Solve problems nonviolently.

⊚ Be aware that we are all part of the same human community.

Part of contributing to a peaceful world is recognizing and respecting people's similarities and differences. Explore the family origins of children in your class. On a world map, locate the countries that the students' families came from. Place their names by the country of their ancestors. You can send a strong message that, though the children have different backgrounds, they are alike in other ways, such as sharing life in the same community and classroom, eating similar foods, listening to popular music, and so on.

Any time of year is the right time to discuss and celebrate diversity. But holiday times in particular are excellent for observing how people around the world gather for festive occasions.

Community of Peacemakers

Help children recognize the important role that peacemakers play around the world. First, children should learn about the qualities that peacemakers possess. Brainstorm these qualities during a community meeting. Peacemakers...

⊚ care about and accept others and themselves

⊚ help others

⊚ are flexible

⊚ try to solve problems and conflicts peacefully and nonviolently

⊚ forgive others

⊚ make compromises

Ask the children: Have you ever served as a peacemaker? Pass around a model of Earth (such as a ball in the shape of Earth). When a child receives it, he or she shares an experience of being a peacemaker. When they use a small globe or Earth-shaped ball, children are reminded that they are part of one planet and that each individual is important to the future of that planet.

Ask: Was it difficult to be a peacemaker? Were there times when it would have been easier not to be? Ask for volunteers to research the United Nations, the American Red Cross, Amnesty International, Doctors Without Borders (winner of the Nobel Peace Prize in 1999), and other humanitarian groups.

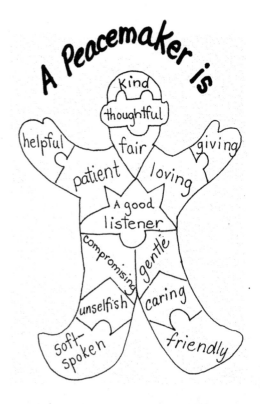

A Peacemaker is
kind
thoughtful
helpful fair giving
patient loving
A good listener
compromising gentle
unselfish caring
soft-spoken friendly

Teaching Kids to Care & Cooperate Scholastic Professional Books

Compile a list of famous peacemakers, past and present. In addition to Abraham Lincoln, Mother Teresa, Martin Luther King Jr., and Jimmy Carter, what other names would you add? Who, for example, is working for peace in Northern Ireland, in the Mideast, in Asia, and in Africa? Suggest that the students award their own Peace Prizes, either to notable peacemakers or to someone in your school or community. Remember that being a peacemaker in your community may mean dealing with matters that are simpler than those of nations, yet just as complex in their own way.

Classmates Near and Far

S taying connected is important for children who, for various reasons, may be out of school. For children who are ill and have to be out for an extended period, classmates can create books, which can be read over and over and treasured during those difficult times. In a fifth-grade classroom a child was ill with cancer. To cheer up their classmate, students designed and wrote a book on emotions. The children brainstormed emotions, then posed as if they were experiencing those feelings. The result was a unique book of photographs that was both humorous and touching.

Send home other kinds of books to keep the sick child connected to his/her classroom life. A traveling journal can go back and forth between the child's home and the school. If the child is too ill to respond, a parent can enter a brief comment or the book can simply be a diary and be returned to the classroom for regular entries.

Don't frown when children must miss regular class time to join their parents on vacations or extended trips. The experience can be a rewarding one for the traveler and for the classmates left behind. Several children's books are tailor-made for this situation. Once you are told of the impending trip, ask your librarian to help you provide the child with a copy of *Learning to Swim in Swaziland: A Child's-eye View of a Southern African Country, Kate Heads West,* or *Let's Go Traveling.* These books recount children's journeys and can serve as models for the traveling child's own reports.

For example, when a fourth grad-

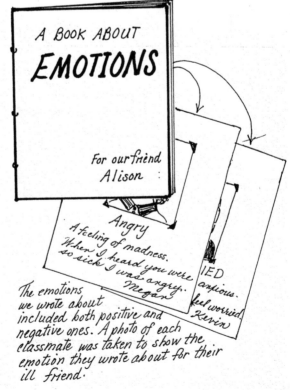

A BOOK ABOUT EMOTIONS

For our friend Alison

Angry
A feeling of madness. When I heard you were so sick I was angry.
Megan

The emotions we wrote about included both positive and negative ones. A photo of each classmate was taken to show the emotion they wrote about for their ill friend.

er recently accompanied her parents to Antarctica, we gave her a copy of *Learning to Swim in Swaziland*. She then created her own travel journal, which she proudly shared with her classmates upon her return. Talk about a geography lesson that was meaningful and exciting for all!

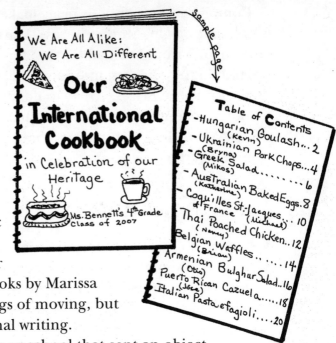

What about the child who moves away? To ease the traumatic feelings that child may be experiencing, the class could give him or her a copy of one of the *Amelia* books by Marissa Moss. Amelia experiences the pangs of moving, but gets some relief through her journal writing.

You may have read about a class or school that sent an object, generally a stuffed toy, out into the community to visit with or travel with a community member. We call ours Travelmate. It travels in a briefcase, durable cloth bag, or small suitcase, accompanied by a journal in which its experiences are recorded.

One year, a third-grade class's Travelmate, a toy dog, provided the students with insights into Germany, Switzerland, Italy, Greece, and Turkey. Travelmate also went to Israel, Florida, Massachusetts, and to children's homes. The children back home followed Travelmate's journey on a map. And when they read the journal on its return, they learned facts about the culture, foods, and traditions of the places it visited that they might never have otherwise.

An ideal book to be shared as you do this activity is *Around the World: Who's Been Here* by Lindsay Barrett George. This book follows the journey of a teacher as she circumnavigates the globe aboard the ship *Explorer* and reports her experiences in photographs, sketches, and letters sent back to her students at home. Compare the teacher's adventures with those of the Travelmate.

No textbook can generate the same level of excitement as Travelmate's postcards, and journal. This project is one more way of allowing families to share in their children's learning, and another means to connect home and school life.

CHAPTER EIGHT

Time to Celebrate

Celebrations—especially those planned and carried out by you and your students—bond the class. Set goals and prepare the groundwork for celebrations so they do not get out of hand or become too broad to be successful. Though holidays are obvious occasions for celebrations, other themes and events provide excuses, too.

UNIT: Science/Rocks and Minerals
CELEBRATION: Rock Exhibit

Students share rock scavenger-hunt results by creating a classroom museum. Display student work from a Rocks and Minerals unit, trade books used as literature connections, and "pet rocks" created as an art project and creative writing lesson. Play rock and roll music! Serve rocky trail mix!

UNIT: Literature/*Charlotte's Web*
CELEBRATION: Charlotte's Web Day

This is a celebration of a great book, *Charlotte's Web*. Students share "book vests" created with their families to recall their memories of the book. Provide paper on which students can send compliments to their classmates about their efforts during this unit. Highlight and discuss qualities of friendship, such as those displayed by the book's characters. As treats, serve spider and pig cupcakes made by the students. Screen the video of the story.

UNIT: Social Studies/the Pilgrims
CELEBRATION: Thanksgiving: Celebration or Harvest Feast

A harvest feast brings together friends and families. It is an ideal time to showcase students' projects completed during the unit. Present choral readings, chants, and a mini-play by students dressed in period clothing. Play colonial games, such as cat's cradle, marbles, and hide-and-seek.

UNIT: Social Studies/Peacemaking
CELEBRATION: Peace Tea

This is a formal performance focusing on poetry, songs, choral readings, and chants prepared and rehearsed by the students. This tea ties together Martin Luther King Jr. Day, Random Acts of Kindness Week, and Valentine's Day. It is a "feel good" show that exemplifies the way people should care for one another.

UNIT: Social Studies/Local or U.S. History
CELEBRATION: Local, County, or State Fairs

Perhaps, there is no better way to celebrate a study's end than to hold a fair. Collect artifacts or pictures that represent significant aspects of your town, state, or nation, such as landmarks, recreational sites, historic areas, and famous residents (past and present). Cook foods representative of your area and compile a recipe book.

As part of the celebration, construct a quilt as a class project. Before you start, the class should brainstorm about what they would like to convey about their topic. Give each child a quilt square (paper or fabric) and ask the child to depict some aspect of the place. Place the squares in a plastic-bag quilt, paste on poster board, or sew them together. If you choose a poster board, attach a crepe paper border to give the quilt a special touch.

State Quilt

Variation

Construct a graduated-pages book called *Reasons Why _____ Is a Great State.* Label each section with a reason why that state is wonderful.

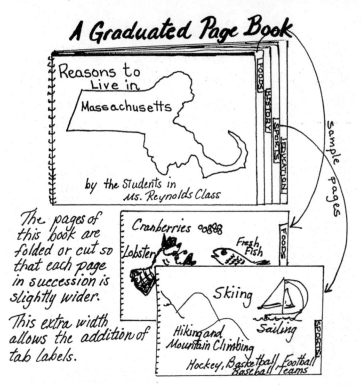

A Graduated Page Book

Reasons to Live in Massachusetts

by the students in Ms. Reynolds Class

The pages of this book are folded or cut so that each page in succession is slightly wider.

This extra width allows the addition of tab labels.

Cranberries Lobster Fresh Fish

Skiing Sailing

Hiking and Mountain Climbing

Hockey, Basketball, Football Baseball Teams

UNIT: Student Writers' Workshop
CELEBRATION: Author's Tea

A festive way to showcase student writing is to hold an authors' tea. The authors in the classroom can invite other classes or their families to listen to their creations. Later, the writers can meet their public and share refreshments.

UNIT: Social Studies/Around the World in 30 Days
CELEBRATION: Music and Art

This activity can be a focus for one month, or can be a year-long multicultural exploration. Before beginning this study, give all students a world map or ask small groups to share one. During the morning announcements, state the name of a country that will be "visited." Ask students to locate that country on a large map or globe. Follow this by having each student locate the country on his/her own map and then trace it with markers or a highlighter. Depending on the amount of time you want to devote to each country, select from a variety of cross-curricular activities.

Art: Display pictures of artwork typical of each country.

Music: Play recordings of native music.

Physical education: Teach games and sports that peoples of that country enjoy.

School wide: Adopt each country for a month and study it in grade-appropriate ways. This study is particularly meaningful during Olympics years.

UNIT: Social Studies/Manners
CELEBRATION: Put Your Best Foot Forward

Students pledge to do their very best in everything—*to put their best foot forward*—on a particular day. Discuss why it's great, but not always possible, to perform to the best of one's ability. On this day, though, everyone should strive for perfection. That's one way to see what would happen if everyone does his/her best for one complete day. Once Best Foot Forward Day is over, ask students to write their reflections in their journals. Did they feel this activity made a difference?

UNIT: Social Studies
CELEBRATION: Birthdays

Birthdays are common classroom celebrations because they are such an important part of children's lives. The book *Birthday a Day* can help the class find out which famous people share their birthdays. This book contains 366 short biographies of people who have made a difference in the world.

Reading this book or other references that list birthdays can motivate students to research others who share their birthday and compile *We Share a Birthday* books. Each could include:

- pictures of the people celebrating the same birthday
- a newspaper headline from the most current birthday
- the weather report from the all-important day
- a local movie listing
- a review of the student's favorite book
- a description of the student's dreams or hopes for the future

In his book *I'm in Charge of Celebrations,* Byrd Baylor beautifully describes the joy of celebrating the wonders of each day, many of which usually go unnoticed. Read this book with your class. Then ask students to help you make a list on the chalkboard of the kinds of celebrations that occur during a year. Include the celebrations described in the book.

Some occasions are personal celebrations—taking part in a piano recital, for example, or making the all-star baseball team, climbing a mountain peak, or spending time at a favorite relative's home. Ask students to write about such a personal experience on an index card. Place these cards in a pocket accordion book. Revisit this book throughout the year, with the children adding or deleting entries.

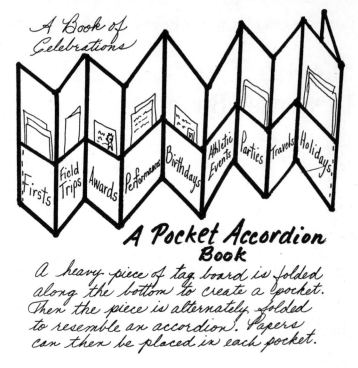

A Book of Celebrations

A Pocket Accordion Book

A heavy piece of tag board is folded along the bottom to create a pocket. Then the piece is alternately folded to resemble an accordion. Papers can then be placed in each pocket.

Firsts · Field Trips · Awards · Performances · Birthdays · Athletic Events · Parties · Travels · Holidays

Pocket Accordion Books

Make one large book or have the children make smaller individual ones.

MATERIALS

☆ long strip of heavyweight paper, wide enough to accommodate an index card (for 3 x 5 cards, the paper must be about ten inches wide)

☆ glue

STEPS

1. If you want more room in the book, glue together several sheets of paper.

2. Turn up the bottom edge of the paper about two inches.

3. Use a paper clip or ruler to score a line along the fold.

4. At about four-inch intervals, score the entire length of the paper, forming little pockets.

5. Insert the cards.

6. The cards are easily removable, so you can use this book for describing personal celebrations, ways to care for Earth, a look at endangered species, acts of kindness, and so on.

Consider celebrating the following days in your classroom!

March 2
Dr. Seuss's Birthday

Across America, people celebrate reading on this day. The goal is for every child in every community to read with an adult. Some special events for this celebration include:

⊚ Hold a *Green Eggs and Ham* party.

⊚ Draw a Dr. Seuss mural.

⊚ Collect and display Dr. Seuss books.

⊚ Graph the different titles and the number of students who own those books. (This can be a class- or schoolwide effort)

⊚ Hold a bedtime read-aloud/pajama party (in the gymnasium).

⊚ Host a family literacy night; show how to effectively read aloud.

⊚ Have a Book Fair for parents to buy books for their children.

⊚ Invite guests to read Dr. Seuss books. Encourage the readers to dress as characters from the books.

⊚ Visit the Seussville web site for games, contests, and fun at www.randomhouse.com/seussville/

The 100th Day

The 100th day of school has become increasingly popular. Generally, this day occurs sometime in February. Here are some activities for your 100th day. Challenge students to make objects that contain 100 items, such as a caterpillar with 100 legs; a doghouse made of 100 dog bones; a straw hat with 100 colorful flowers; a scrapbook with 100 pictures of the student; a cardboard or wooden "soda bottle" with 100 soda caps.

⊚ Read books that have 100 as part of their story, such as *The Hundred Dresses, 100 Hungry Ants, One Hundred is a Family.*

⊚ Collect samples of 100 acts of kindness.

⊚ Collect 100 cans of food to donate to a food pantry.

⊚ Invite a 100-year-old person to the class for an interview.

⊚ Construct 100 hearts, each with a message about creating a better world or with expressions of thankfulness.

- Give each student $100 in play money. Distribute newspaper circulars from which the children can "buy" $100 worth of items.

- Have the students send 100 e-mail messages and mark their destinations on a map.

Math Month/Family Math Night

Celebrate the mathematics program in your school. Designate one month as Math Month and schedule a variety of activities. End with a Family Math Night. Some Math Month suggestions:

- Read a variety of children's literature that has a math focus.

- Keep math journals.

- Make tangrams.

- Place an estimating jar in the main foyer; have children estimate the amount of items in the jar.

- Keep a water fountain tally; place tally marks on a chart each time a student takes a drink.

- Sort buttons and create button pictures.

- Go comparison shopping using newspaper circulars.

Poetry Month

April is National Poetry Month, a wonderful opportunity to make poetry teaching come alive in the classroom. Start each day by reading poems by various poets over the public address system or in your room. Compile poems by students in a poetry anthology that can be shared with others in the community and donated to the class, school, or public library. If you like, dedicate a Poet of the Week bulletin board. Assign a student committee to be in charge, to change the board once a week, to solicit suggestions from classmates and other teachers, and to choose the honored poet. Then try these fun poetry ideas:

- Create shape poetry.

- Write and illustrate poems about colors and feelings.

- Create an anthology of calendar poems.

- Read or listen to poems and draw interpretations.

- Staple a pocket taken from an old pair of jeans onto cardboard or a thin piece of wood. Insert poems into the pockets.

- On the front of manila envelopes, paste or draw different poetry topics, such as the weather, mountains, or circus animals. Find appropriate poems to place inside.

- Place in your poetry corner a tape recorder and recordings of poets reading their works or of students reading poems.

- Attach real or paper branches to a bulletin board to serve as display areas for poems. Tape poems to the branches.

- Create a poetry-book display area.

THE Poet tree

Poems are copied on 3x5 index cards and placed in the pockets on the tree.

Celebrate Book-Award Winners

Some of the awards that annually honor quality children's literature are the Caldecott Award (for best picture book), the Newbery Award (for best novel), and the Coretta Scott King Award (for best African-American contribution). Plan your own awards celebrations. Display winning books. Use *A Caldecott Celebration: Six Artists and Their Paths to the Caldecott Medal* as a model for this celebration. Invite your students to research the authors and illustrators of the award-winning books, and post findings on a bulletin board outside the school library.

The Great Nutrition Adventure

National Nutrition Month is in March; Children's Book Week is in April; American Education Week is in November. The Great Nutrition Adventure, which celebrates food and nutrition by pairing a week's breakfasts and lunches with children's favorite books, can be any time. This excellent activity promotes healthy eating *and* encourages literacy skills. The students are encouraged to read books, discuss nutrition, and enjoy the meals. Food-related books could include: *Gregory the Terrible Eater* by Mitchell Sharmot; *Strega Nona* by Tomie DePaola; *Milk Makers* by Gail Gibbons; *Cloudy With a Chance of Meatballs* by Judi Barrett; *Chicken Soup With Rice* by Maurice Sendak; and *Green Eggs and Ham* by Dr. Seuss.

The Olympics

The Summer and Winter Olympics present a golden opportunity to provide students with a global perspective. The Winter Olympics falls during the school year and can be easily incorporated into the curriculum, whereas the Summer Olympics typically occurs when American schools are on summer vacation. However, it too can be explored in June with a schoolwide Field Day as the culminating activity. During the Olympics study, a museum of artifacts from around the world can be created and displayed in the library, hallways, and in classrooms. Students can serve as tour guides.

Celebrate Children

In June 1996, Marian Wright Edelman, the president and cofounder of the Children's Defense Fund, held a rally at the Lincoln Memorial in Washington, D.C. She encouraged people everywhere to" stand for children." Since that time, June 1st has been observed as a day for Americans to confirm their commitment to children. A version of Edelman's speech, with its message of hope, has been turned into a powerful picture book, *Stand for Children,* which is illustrated with quilts of fabrics and photographs. The book states that "Each and every American child adds or subtracts, multiplies or divides America's problems and potential, and fulfills America's nightmares or dreams."

Year-End Performances

The children have summer vacation to anticipate, but they must also say their good-byes to the community to which they have grown attached.

Presenting class performances can be one way to celebrate the year's end and help students with transitions. Here are some of the tasks to do to prepare for the performance of the year.

1. Choose a date. Make it realistic. There's a lot of work to be done.

2. Choose a theme based on a major topic or unit that the class has worked on.

3. Assign a committee, or decide as a group what you would like to do. You

could sing songs, recite poetry, or present a play. If you choose to do the latter, decide who will write the script.

4. Ask students to write letters to family members and neighbors to solicit help and support in constructing props and scenery, working on scripts at home, transporting children to and from the performance, providing refreshments, and so on.

5. Solicit donations from the community. Ask for technical assistance, prop loans, and permission to display posters advertising the performance in shop windows, supermarkets, and apartment buildings.

6. Invite community members to your classroom to speak about the theme of the production to give it more meaning. For example, when Alice's school underwent a major construction project one year, the class theme was construction. Construction workers spoke to the class about their jobs.

Taking part in performances is an educational experience. Students memorize parts, cooperate to design scenery and props, practice public speaking, learn about acting and the theater, and work toward a common goal. They also come to respect one another's work and the part everyone plays in creating the whole performance. Performances afford an opportunity for the children to be involved in situations where they must show self-control, self-discipline, and appropriate skills.

Once the preparations are completed, invite the entire community to the gala event. Students' performances are well received and provide wonderful closure to a year of hard work. They bring people together to *celebrate* children!

Growing Together

Each of the sudents in Lisa Riley's third-grade class draw trees that are hung in the hallway outside their classroom. A poem related to the month or theme being explored is hung on the tree along with a positive comment about the child. Then self-esteem building notes are added to the tree every month; the child and the tree "grow" together throughout the year.

Another end-of-the-year activity is constructing a final quilt—an autograph quilt. To construct this quilt, place your name and the school year in the center of quilt squares. The students collect autographs from all their classmates. In the corners of the squares, the students write some special memories of the year.

Corkstrip Quilt

Corkstrip Quilt

If time is a factor, or if you'd prefer a flexible quilt format, make a corkstrip quilt. To make this quilt, buy corkstrips and attach them to a wall, with the spacing wide enough to accommodate standard-size paper. Alternate quilt blocks made of decorative wallpaper with the students' contributions. Because they are attached with thumbtacks, the quilt squares are easily changeable. The wallpaper squares can remain for the entire year, or can also be changed.

Have a quilt show as your final celebration for the year. Display all quilts you made—mementos of the learning and caring that took place in your room throughout the year. Invite visitors to see the quilts. You could give each quilt a blue ribbon for Best of Show. All the children had a hand in all the quilts, so they are all winners!

Hang corkstrip pieces at equal distances to display standard-size sheets (8 or 10 inches apart for 8x10 sheets) Alternate pieces of wallpaper or wrapping paper as contrasting quilt blocks.

About Me

My name is _____

My birthday is _____

I'm special because _____

I like to _____

_____

I'm good at _____

_____

_____

I'd like to do better at _____

_____

_____

My favorite time at school is when _____

_____

If I could have three wishes, I would ask for:

   1. _____

   2. _____

   3. _____

My favorite book is _____

I like this book because _____

_____

A Note From Your Child's Teacher

We are studying measurement and will be making books to share what we've learned. To help us get started, each child needs to do some measuring at home. Please help your child with this assignment.

Child's Notes:

1. Measure your favorite toy. Toy name: _____

   Length in inches: _____ in centimeters: _____

2. Find an object that is the same length as your favorite toy. It is a

   _____

3. How many pieces of your favorite cereal fill one cup? _____ pieces

4. What is the temperature outside?

   Date: _____ _____ degrees

5. What is your height? _____ feet _____ inches

6. What is your weight? _____ pounds

7. How long is your foot? _____ inches

8. Find the weight of the following items:

Type	Name	Weight
A box of pasta		
A small bag of flour or sugar		
A small bottle of water, juice, or soda		
A medium-size can		

9. How long is your toothbrush? _____ inches

10. How long is a piece of fruit? Type _____ Length _____ inches

11. Find the distance (in miles) it takes to get from your home to somewhere else.

    I went to _____ from my house.

    It was _____ miles.

RIGHTS	RESPONSIBILITIES
You have the right to...	**and the responsibility to...**
be safe and have your belongings be safe.	treat other people's property appropriately and with care.
work in a quiet place.	work quietly and not disturb others.
be treated fairly.	treat others fairly.
work in a clean room.	keep the room clean and pick up after yourself.
use school materials and equipment.	share school materials and equipment.
be heard and have your opinions respected.	listen to other's opinions thoughtfully and respectfully.
study and learn.	study and learn.
make mistakes without being criticized.	let others make mistakes without making fun of them.
socialize with friends.	keep socializing from interfering with your learning and your classmates' learning.
be respected.	respect others.

WE ALL MAKE CHOICES

A Winner will say...	A Loser will say...
I'll try.	no.
let's do it.	I don't want to.
I'm getting better.	I'm terrible at this.
maybe there's another way.	this doesn't work.
let's ask for help	I quit.
give someone else a turn.	I had it first.
you can join us.	there's no room.
that was a good try.	it stinks.

WINNERS AND LOSERS

A Winner...	A Loser...
uses time wisely.	wastes time.
tries harder.	quits easily.
helps others.	refuses to help others.
gives compliments.	uses put downs.
focuses on the positive.	focuses on the negative.
admits mistakes.	blames others.
is dependable.	can't be depended on.
succeeds.	fails.
shows appreciation.	ignores others' contributions.
puts forth best effort.	doesn't try.

My Trip to Antarctica

by Carole Lewis (Grade 4)

Down at the bottom of the Earth is a large, cold, white continent…Antarctica! On December 5, my father, mother, and I left our house and spent more than one day traveling to Santiago, Chile. There we spent two hot days touring the city and countryside. On the third day, we took a plane to Punta Arenas, which is at the southern tip of Chile. We boarded our ship, the Caledonian Star, along with 84 other passengers. After the anchor was lifted, we started our voyage to Antarctica.

We sailed down and around Cape Horn, where we saw our first penguins, the Magellanic. They were one of seven different kinds of penguins we saw on the trip. Then we traveled through the dangerous Drake Passage (dangerous because of rough seas and high winds). We made it safely to the South Shetland Islands, which are located in Antarctica. In Antarctica, we saw a lot more penguins, seals, seabirds, icebergs, glaciers, and sleeping volcanoes.

After 8 days of exploring Antarctica's shoreline and islands, our ship left for the South Orkney Islands and South Georgia Island. There, we visited a large abandoned whaling station. We saw many kinds of albatross, reindeer, fur and elephant seals, and whales.

We next sailed rough seas for three days to get to the Falkland Islands. The Islands were very windy, rocky, and seemed crowded with sheep—not people. The capital is Port Stanley and is about the size of Cambridge, N.Y. We boarded a plane there and flew back to Santiago. The next day we left for home, arriving on New Year's Eve.

One of the hardest things we did was to be at sea on Christmas. One of the best things about the trip was watching and walking among the penguins. Going to Antarctica was a great experience for me. I learned many things and met interesting people from all around the world. I hope to go back to Antarctica someday and be with the penguins again.

Thoughts About Peace Tea

by _____

Today we will videotape our performance. How do you feel about that?

_____

_____

What is your favorite part of our performance (not counting refreshments)?

_____

_____

What part of our performance do we do BEST?

_____

_____

What do you think is the audience's favorite part?

_____

_____

How do you think the _____ graders will feel coming back to this class to see the performance today?

_____

_____

How do you feel about performing for the _____ graders?

_____

_____

Why? _____

_____

Countdown to Earth Day

April 22 is Earth Day. To help celebrate, use your imagination to think of one or two new uses for each of the following items. Write your ideas in the boxes below.

1. Milk carton	**2.** Old sock	**3.** Comics section in the newspaper
4. Decorative gift bag	**5.** Cereal box	**6.** Plastic laundry-soap scoop
7. Puzzle pieces	**8.** Egg carton	**9.** Old envelopes
10. Catalogs	**11.** Map	**12.** Ice cream sticks
13. Resealable plastic bag	**14.** Film container	**15.** Shoe box
16. Old book	**17.** Muffin tin	**18.** Old watch
19. Paper plate	**20.** Elastic bands	**21.** Aluminum can

Happy Earth Day!

Teaching Kids to Care & Cooperate Scholastic Professional Books

BOOKS FOR CHILDREN

Many of these books are useful in more than one category. The starred (*) books are those we especially recommend.

Getting to Know Ourselves and One Another

ABC I Like Me by Nancy Carlson (Viking, 1997). The narrator uses the alphabet to celebrate herself.

All About Me: A Keepsake Journal for Kids by Linda Kranz (Northland Publishing, 1996). Colorful illustrations and thought-starters guide children in selecting ideas to write about.

Amelia's Notebook by Marissa Moss (Tricycle Press, 1995). In her journal, a nine-year-old records her thoughts about moving, school, her sister, her best friend, and a new friend.

Around the World: Who's Been There by Lindsay Barrett George (Greenwillow Books, 1999). A teacher, viewing animals in their natural habitats around the world, writes to her class.

For Your Eyes Only! by Joanne Rocklin (Scholastic, 1997). Sixth graders' journal entries reveal their feelings and lives.

Glad Monster, Sad Monster by Anne Miranda (Little, Brown, 1997). This is a book about feelings.

If You're Not From the Prairie by David Bouchard (Simon & Schuster, 1995). A boy grows up on the prairie.

It's Raining Laughter by Nikki Grimes (Dial, 1997). Poems that deal with growing up.

Just Because I Am, A Child's Book of Affirmations by Lauren Payne (Free Spirit Publishing, 1994). Strengthening a child's self-esteem.

Kate Heads West by Pat Brisson (Bradbury Press, 1990). In letters to friends and relatives, Kate describes her trip.

Learning to Swim in Swaziland: A Child's-eye View of a Southern African Country by Nila Leigh (Scholastic, 1993). An eight-year-old girl describes her year living in Swaziland.

Let's Go Traveling by Robin Rector Krupp (Morrow Junior Books, 1992). Using a variety of formats, a girl writes about a journey.

Marianthe's Story One: Painted Words and *Marianthe's Story Two: Spoken Memories* by Aliki (Greenwillow Books, 1998). One book tells of a girl's life in a Greek village; the second has two separate stories about her new life in America.

Measuring Penny by Loreen Leedy (Henry Holt and Company, 1997). There are many ways to measure a dog.

Rope Burn by Jan Siebold (Whitman, 1998). The assignment is to use a proverb to explain a significant event.

Sometimes I Feel Like a Mouse: A Book About Feelings by Jeanne Modesitt (Scholastic, 1992). Why it is important to respect others' feelings.

Somewhere Today by Shelley Thomas (Whitman, 1998). People bringing about peace by caring for one another.

Voices of the Heart by Ed Young (Scholastic, 1997). Exploring 26 Chinese characters that describe a feeling or emotion.

Routines and Rules

☆ To start off a discussion of classroom rules and behavior, try *Miss Nelson Is Missing* by Harry Allard and James Marshall. Miss Nelson's classroom tends to be a little unruly until a substitute teacher, Viola Swamp, straightens it out. Her situation could frame a discussion of how her students—like yours—could learn to cooperate and behave appropriately. (Houghton Mifflin, 1985)

☆ Stanley, the hero of the Newbery Award-winning *Holes* by Louis Sachar, has been sent to a detention camp located in a parched wasteland. As a student he had not been liked and had not found a sense of belonging in his school. To exist at the camp, he has succeeded in learning acceptable behaviors. Your upper-grade students could discuss Stanley's plight, both at his school and at the camp, and make connections to the community they are establishing in their own classroom. Talking about fiction in this way focuses on issues that do not *directly* relate to the students themselves; it defuses emotional situations that might seem too personal if you approach them directly. (Farrar, Straus and Giroux, 1998)

☆ For the lower grades, picture books are invaluable for initiating discussions before developing rules for the year. *The Butter Battle Book* by Dr. Seuss (Random House, 1984) shows how conflicts can get out of hand. *Alexander and the Terrible, Horrible, No Good, Very Bad Day* by Judith Viorst with illustrations by Ray Cruz (Antheneum, 1972) helps children think of appropriate ways to handle a not-so-wonderful day.

The Awful Aardvarks Go to School by Reeve Lindberg (Viking, 1997). An alphabetical listing of the destruction committed by mischievous aardvarks during a visit to school.

Benny and the No-Good Teacher by Cheryl Zach (Macmillan, 1992). Benny looks forward to fourth grade until he meets his new teacher.

Berenstein's Bears' Trouble at School by Stan Berenstein and Jan Berenstein (Random House, 1986). Brother Bear learns the consequences of neglecting responsibilities.

Dear God, Help! Love, Earl by Barbara Park (Alfred A. Knopf, 1993). Wimpy Earl avoids the class bully.

Don't Go to the Principal's Office by M. Coffin (Avon, 1996). What terrors lurk behind the new principal's door?

Dress Code Mess by Sara St. Antoine (Bantam Books, 1992). Lenni contests her school's dress code.

How to Survive Third Grade by Laurie Lawlor (Pocket Books, 1988). An unpopular third grader has a hard time until he finds a friend and experiences his first real successes.

Miss Yonkers Goes Bonkers by Mike Thaler (Avon, 1994). It's no ordinary day when the principal wears a chicken suit and Miss Yonkers outdoes the worst student behavior.

Rose Swanson: Fourth-Grade Geek for President by Barbara Park (Alfred A. Knopf, 1992). With the help of her fellow nerds, Rosie is determined to win the school election.

Spitball Class by Candice Ransom (Pocket Books, 1994). How will Austin survive as the newest student in the worst class?

There's a Boy in the Girls' Bathroom by Louis Sachar (Alfred A. Knopf, 1987). An 11-year-old misfit learns to believe in himself.

Caring for One Another

☆ Help students in the lower grades understand the concept of community from the start of the school year. *Whoever You Are* by Mem Fox is a perfect discussion starter about respecting one another and appreciating diversity. (Harcourt, 1997)

☆ Children in the middle and upper grades will get plenty of food for thought from *The Green Book* by Jill Paton Walsh. It is about Earthlings who leave their planet because of a catastrophe. They travel on a spaceship, carrying a few treasured items and some practical objects, such as tools. Once they reach their destination, the refugees have to establish a new community, design rules, divide responsibilities, and ensure the settlers' safety. This is an excellent story that can help children envision the ramifications of starting a society. (Farrar Straus & Giroux, 1979)

101 Tips for Being a Best Friend by Nancy Krulik (Scholastic, 1997). Everything anyone needs to know about making and keeping a best friend.

A Teacher Is a Special Person by Bernard Farber (Peter Pauper Press, 1996). We know this is true! Here's a thoughtful tribute.

Fritz and the Beautiful Horses by Jan Brett (Houghton Mifflin, 1981). A pony excluded from a herd of beautiful horses becomes a hero.

Helping Out is Cool by Ellen Moss (Tumbleweed Press, 1997). Why service to others is important.

Love Your Neighbor: Stories of Values and Virtues by Arthur Dobrin (Scholastic, 1999). Imaginative animal fables offer thought-provoking life lessons to share with children.

Mufaro's Beautiful Daughters by John Steptoe (Lothrop, Lee, & Shepard, 1987). Mufaro's two daughters, one evil and one sweet, go before the king who is choosing a bride.

Random Acts of Kindness, Kids' Random Acts of Kindness, More Random Acts of Kindness, The Community of Kindness (Conari Press: 1993, 1994, 1999). How people can make a real difference through kindness and building community. Also: *Peaceful Kingdom: Random Acts of Kindness by Animals* by Stephanie LaLand (1997).

Simple Acts of Kindness by Ray Alonzo (Trade Life Books, 1998). Little actions can make a difference.

Tattercoats by J. Jacobs (G.P. Putnam's Sons, 1989). This Cinderella story depicts unfair treatment of the heroine.

The Doorbell Rang by Pat Hutchins (Morrow, 1990). Each time the doorbell rings, more children want some wonderful cookies.

The Little Red Hen by Harriet Ziefert (Viking, 1995). Her lazy friends won't help, so an ambitious hen makes bread by herself.

The Rainbow Fish by Morris Pfister (North South Books, 1992). The most beautiful fish learns about friendship and sharing.

The Talking Eggs by Robert San Souci (Dial, 1989). A southern version of Cinderella.

Willie's Not the Hugging Kind by Joyce Barrett (HarperCollins, 1989). Willie's best friend thinks hugs are silly.

Beyond the Classroom

☆ *Will We Miss Them?: Endangered Species* was written by Alexandra Wright when she was 11 years old. Each page begins with the question, *Will we miss them?*, then adds the name of an endangered species, such as, *Will we miss the grizzly bear?* Information about and illustrations of each animal follow each question. The book ends with a plea for children to find out about endangered species, to let others know about them, and to be proactive about their plight. As the author says, "If we all care, we can make our world a place where people and animals can live together in harmony." (Charlesbridge Publishing, 1993)

Anthology for the Earth by Judy Allen (Candlewick Press, 1998). Stories from many cultures in defense of Earth.

Common Ground: The Water, Earth, and Air We Share by Molly Bang (Scholastic, 1997). Here is a point of reference about modern environmental problems facing the world.

Earth Day by Linda Lowery (Carolrhoda Books, 1991). How the annual Earth Day celebration started and activities to call global attention to environment problems.

The Earth Is Good: A Chant in Praise of Nature by Michale DeMunn (Scholastic, 1999). A Native American conservationist affirms the goodness of life.

Earthsong by Sally Rogers (Dutton, 1998). This book introduces endangered species using the song "Over in the Meadow" as a pattern.

Gifts by Phyllis Tildes (Charlesbridge, 1997). In this rhyming story, a young girl encounters the gifts nature has to offer.

Giving Thanks: A Native American Good Morning Message by Chief Jake Swamp (Lee & Low, 1995). A contemporary Mohawk chief draws on the Six Nation ceremonial tradition in a thanks offering to Mother Earth.

The Giving Tree by Shel Silverstein (Harcourt, 1964). An apple tree shares all it has with a human from the time he is a child though his old age.

Going Green: A Kid's Handbook to Saving the Planet by John Elkington, Julia Hailes, Douglas Hill and Joel Makower (Puffin Books, 1990). Ways children can protect the Earth.

Happy Birthday, Martin Luther King by Jean Marzollo (Scholastic, 1993). The story of the civil rights hero.

The Hunterman and the Crocodile by Baba Diakite (Scholastic, 1997). A West African hunter man learns the importance of living in harmony with nature.

If I Were in Charge of the World and Other Worries by Judith Viorst (Aladdin, 1981). Forty-one poems reveal a variety of thoughts, worries, and wishes.

Jaguarundi by Virginia Hamilton. (Scholastic, 1995). Twelve endangered rain forest animals struggle to find a habitat.

This Land Is Your Land by Woody Guthrie (Little, Brown, 1998). Based on the Guthrie song, the words and illustrations create a portrait of our diverse land and people.

Lester & Clyde by James Reece (Scholastic, 1976). The story of two frogs whose pristine environment is spoiled by pollution.

Long Live the Earth by Megan Morrison (Scholastic, 1993). This tale, illustrated with quilt blocks, reflects on what people have done to Earth and carries a message of hope.

The Lorax by Dr. Seuss (Random House, 1971). The Once-ler describes the results of the local pollution problem.

The Story of Ruby Bridges by Robert Coles (Scholastic, 1995). Children's spirit of courage and forgiveness highlights this true story of the first black student, a six-year-old girl, at an all-white elementary school.

This Is the Sea That Feeds Us by Robert Baldwin (Dawn, 1998). The ocean is one big food chain.

V for Vanishing: An Alphabet of Endangered Species by Patricia Mullins (Harcourt, 1993). This beautifully illustrated book depicts threatened animals around the world.

Window by Jeannie Baker (Puffin Books, 1991). An unspoiled environment becomes polluted in this text-free picture book.

The Wump World by Bill Peet (Houghton Mifflin, 1970). The Wump World is an unspoiled place until huge monsters bring hordes of tiny creatures from the planet Pollutus.

Problem Solving and Conflict Resolution

☆ *The Big Book for PEACE*, edited by Ann Durell and Marilyn Sachs, is a compilation of stories, illustrations, pictures, songs, and poems about peace by more than 30 distinguished authors and illustrators. The book can serve as a springboard for children to write about and illustrate what they think peace means. (Dutton Children's Books, 1990)

The Best Way to Play, The Meanest Thing to Say, Shipwreck Saturday, The Treasure Hunt by Bill Cosby (Scholastic, 1997, 1998). Discovering your own special and unique talents.

The Bomb and the General by Umberto Eco and Eurgenio Carmi (Harcourt Brace, 1989). A plea for an end to all wars.

Donkey Trouble by Ed Young (Aladdin, 1995). In this traditional fable, a man and his grandson, on their way to market with their donkey, find it impossible to please everyone they meet.

The Hating Book by Charlotte Zolotow (HarperCollins, 1969). Two former friends hate each other until a mistake is cleared up.

How to Be a Friend by Laurie Brown (Little, Brown, 1998). A guide to making friends and keeping them.

The Island of Skog by Steven Kellogg (Dial, 1973). To escape the dangers of urban life, Jenny and her friends sail to an island, only to be faced with its only inhabitant, the Skog.

Make Someone Smile and 40 More Ways to Be a Peaceful Person by Douglas Mason-Fry (Free Spirit, 1996). It's not hard to teach one another to listen, think, compromise, smile, and celebrate.

A Million Visions of Peace by Jennifer Garrison (Pfeifer-Hamilton, 1996). Children and adults from every state express their desire for a more peaceful world.

Old Turtle by Douglas Wood (Pfiefer-Hamilton, 1992). This moving fable promotes a deeper understanding of Earth.

Self-help and Advice

Brother Eagle, Sister Sky: A Message from Chief Seattle by Susan Jeffers (Dial, 1991). The words of the legendary Chief Seattle capture the central belief of Native Americans, the sacredness of Earth.

In a Sacred Manner I Live: Native American Wisdom edited by Neil Philip (Houghton Mifflin, 1997). A collection of speeches by Native Americans.

Life's Little Instruction Book (several volumes) by H. Jackson Brown Jr. (Rutledge Hill Press). Originally fatherly advice to a college-bound son, these best-sellers offer suggestions and observations about living a rewarding life.

My Wish for Tomorrow (William Morrow, 1995). A compilation of children's words in honor of the UN's 50th anniversary.

Really Important Stuff My Kids Have Taught Me by Cynthia Lewis (Workman Publishing, 1994). Funny, smart, and sensible things the author's children have taught her.

Seuss-isms: Wise and Witty Prescriptions for Living From the Good Doctor by Dr. Seuss (Random House, 1997). A collection.

A Sip of Aesop by Jane Yolen (Scholastic, 1995). Aesop's fables in verse.

Celebrations

A Calendar of Festivals by Cherry Gilchrist (Barefoot Books, 1998). The origins and stories of world-wide festivals.

Celebrate the Spirit: The Olympic Games by Cleve Dheensaw and Deanna Binder (Orca Press, 1996). A comprehensive Olympic history.

Celebrating Hanukkah by Diane Hoyt-Goldsmith (Holiday House, 1993). Color photographs illustrate the traditions of Hanukkah, as it is observed by a Jewish family in San Francisco.

Celebrating Kwanzaa by Diane Hoyt-Goldsmith (Holiday House, 1996). A photo essay shows how one family celebrates Kwanzaa.

Celebration! by Jane Resh Thomas (Warner Books, 1997). Grandmother, aunts, uncles, and cousins gather for a family picnic.

Celebrations by Jerry Craven (Rourke Press, 1996). The rituals that mark special days in a person's life, such as birthdays, name days, bar mitzvahs, and marriages.

Celebrations Around the World: A Multicultural Handbook by Carole Angell (Fulcrum Publishing, 1996). A multicultural resource for celebrations and festivals.

Celebrations of Light: A Year of Holidays Around the World by Nancy Luenn (Simon & Schuster, 1998). In this multicultural collection, light is the unifying theme.

Celebrating America: A Collection of Poems and Images of the American Spirit by Laura Whipple (Putnam, 1994). Poems honor the American people.

Celebrating the Powwow by Bobbie Kalman (Crabtree, 1997). An examination of the North American powwow, its preparations, competitions, traditional costumes, and symbols.

Festivals of the World: England by Harlinah Whyte (Gareth Stevens Publishing, 1997). How England's culture is reflected in its festivals, including Guy Fawkes Day, the Notting Hill Carnival, and Lord Mayor's Day.

I'm In Charge of Celebrations by Byrd Baylor (Aladdin, 1986). A desert dweller celebrates a triple rainbow, a chance encounter with a coyote, and other wonders of the wilderness.

Let the Celebrations Begin! by Margaret Wild (Orchard Books, 1991). Memories of celebrations at home sustain a child in a World War II German concentration camp.

Let's Celebrate: Festival Poems by John Foster (Oxford University Press, 1989). A multicultural poetry collection celebrating festivals around the world.

The Penny Whistle: Any Day Is a Holiday Book by Meredith Brokaw, Annie Gilbar, and Jill Weber (Simon & Schuster, 1996). Ideas for activities, decorations, and food for parties.

Quilts

A Cloak for the Dreamer by Aileen Friedman (Scholastic, 1995). A tailor asks his three sons to make a cloak for the archduke.

Cemetery Quilt by Kent Ross and Alice Ross (Houghton Mifflin, 1995). Her family's cemetery quilt convinces a girl to attend her grandfather's funeral.

Coat of Many Colors by Dolly Parton (HarperCollins, 1994). A poor girl is happy with her coat made from rags by her mother because she knows the coat was made with love.

Bess's Log Cabin Quilt by Anne Love (Holiday House, 1995). With her father away and her mother ill, a young girl works hard on making a log-cabin quilt to save the family farm.

The Canada Geese Quilt by Natalie Kinsey-Warnock (Dodd, Mead, 1988). Worried that a new baby and her grandmother's illness will change her family's life, a young girl makes a special quilt.

Earth Day by Linda Lowery (Carolrhoda Books, 1991). How the annual Earth Day celebration started, and activities to call global attention to environment problems.

Eight Hands Round: A Patchwork Alphabet by Ann Paul (HarperCollins, 1991). Using the alphabet, this book explains the origins of early American patchwork quilt patterns.

Elmer: The Story of a Patchwork Elephant by David McKee (McGraw-Hill, 1968). All the elephants are gray except Elmer, who is a patchwork of colors, until he tires of being different.

The Josefina Story Quilt by Eleanor Coerr (Harper & Row, 1986). Traveling west in 1850, a girl makes a quilt telling of the experiences; she saves a special patch for her pet hen, Josefina.

The Keeping Quilt by Patricia Polacco (Simon & Schuster, 1988). A homemade quilt links the lives of four generations of an immigrant Jewish family, remaining a symbol of love and faith.

Luka's Quilt by Georgia Guback (Greenwillow Books, 1994). Luka is initially disappointed in the quilt her grandmother made for her, but eventually the two settle their differences.

My Grandmother's Patchwork Quilt: A Book and Pocketful of Patchwork Pieces by Janet Bolton (Doubleday, 1994). Alternating pages describe a young girl's life on a farm and how she constructed a quilt to capture memories of that life. Includes ten quilt squares so readers can make their own quilts.

Osa's Pride by Ann Grifalconi (Little, Brown, 1990). Osa's grandmother tells her a story about the sins of pride and helps Osa gain a perspective on what is really important.

94

Teaching Kids to Care & Cooperate Scholastic Professional Books

Patchwork Island by Karla Kuskin.(HarperCollins, 1994). A mother stitches the varied topography of their beautiful island into her patchwork pattern while making a quilt for her child.

The Patchwork Quilt by Valerie Flournoy (Dial, 1985). Using scraps cut from her family's old clothing, an African-American girl helps her grandmother and mother make a quilt.

The Pumpkin Blanket by Deborah Zagwyn (Celestial Arts, 1990). A child sacrifices her blanket to save pumpkins from frost.

The Quilt Story by Tony Johnston (Putnam, 1985). A pioneer mother stitches a quilt for her daughter; years later another mother patches it for her little girl.

The Rag Coat by Lauren Mills (Little, Brown, 1991). Minna proudly wears her new coat made of clothing scraps; when the children make fun of her, she tells them about each scrap.

Sam Johnson and the Blue Ribbon Quilt by Lisa Ernst (Lothrop, Lee, & Shepard, 1983). While mending an awning, Sam discovers that he enjoys sewing the patches together but meets with scorn when he asks his wife if he could join her quilting group.

Shota and the Star Quilt by Christine Fowler (Zero to Ten Ltd, 1998). Set in Minneapolis, this modern story examines an age-old theme— the triumph of love over power and greed.

Stand for Children by Marian Wright Edelman (Hyperion Books for Children, 1998). Multilayered quilts illustrate the inspiring words of a speech delivered at a rally at the Lincoln Memorial.

Stitching Stars: The Story Quilts of Harriet Powers by Mary Lyons (Charles Scribner's Sons, 1993). Varied quilts are featured in this biography of an African-American quilter.

A Stitch in Time, and its sequel *Broken Days,* by Ann Rinaldi (Scholastic 1994, 1995). Historical novels set in Salem, Massachusetts.

Sweet Clara and the Freedom Quilt by Deborah Hopkinson (Knopf, 1993). A young slave stitches a quilt with a map pattern that guides her to freedom.

Tar Beach by Faith Ringold (Crown, 1991). Based on the author's quilt painting, this story is about a young girl who dreams of flying above her Harlem home.

Texas Star by Barbara Cole (Orchard Books, 1990). Although Papa grumbles about his family needing another quilt, he is only too happy to use it after the quilting bee.

Tonight Is Carnaval by Arthur Dorros (Dutton, 1991). A boy prepares for carnival time in Peru.

The Whispering Cloth: A Refugee's Story by Pegi Shea (Boyds Mills Press, 1995). A girl in a Thai refugee camp creates her own pa'ndau.

BOOKS FOR TEACHERS

A Book of One's Own: Developing Literacy Through Making Books by Paul Johnson (Heinemann, 1990)

Books Don't Have to Be Flat: Innovative Ways to Publish Students' Writing in Every Curriculum by Kathy Pike and Jean Mumper (Scholastic, 1998)

Building Character & Community in the Classroom by Rick Duvall (Creative Teaching Press, 1997)

Cooperative Quilts: Classroom Quilts for the Entire School Year by Diane Bonica and Kathy Devlin (Fearon Teacher Aids, 1997)

Creating a Caring Classroom: Hundreds of Practical Ways to Make It Happen by Nancy Letts (Scholastic, 1997)

Creating Your Classroom Community by Lois Bridges (Stenhouse Publishers, 1995)

Dealing with Dilemmas: Coaching Students in Decision Making by Mark Meyers and Doyle Casteel (A Good Year Book, 1999)

Do You Know What Tomorrow Is? by Lee Bennett Hopkins and Misha Arenstein (Scholastic, 1990)

The Friendly Classroom for a Small Planet by Priscilla Prutzman, Lee Stern, Leonard Burger, and Gretchen Bodenhamer (New Society Publishers, 1988)

Joining Hands: From Personal to Planetary Friendship in the Primary Classroom by Rahima Wade (Zephyr Press, 1991)

Quilting Activities Across the Curriculum by Wendy Buchberg (Scholastic, 1996)

Quilts by Susan Zimmerman (Teacher Created Materials, 1996)

Ready, Set, Cooperate by Marlene Barron (John Wiley & Sons, 1996)

Teaching Conflict Resolution through Children's Literature by William Kreidler (Scholastic, 1994)

Thinking and Learning Together: Curriculum and Community in a Primary Classroom by Bobbi Fisher (Heinemann, 1995)

This Planet Is Mine by Dianna Damkoehler (Scholastic, 1995)